Intentional Grandparenting

Intentional Grandparenting

A BOOMeR'S GUidE

Peggy Edwards and Mary Jane Sterne

M&S

Library and Archives Canada Cataloguing in Publication

Edwards, Peggy
Intentional grandparenting: a boomer's guide / Peggy Edwards & Mary Jane Sterne.

ISBN 0-7710-3052-5

1. Grandparenting. 2. Grandparent and child. I. Title.

HQ759.9.E39 2005   306.874'5   C2004-906725-7

We acknowledge the financial support of the Government of Canada through the Book Publishing Industry Development Program and that of the Government of Ontario through the Ontario Media Development Corporation's Ontario Book Initiative. We further acknowledge the support of the Canada Council for the Arts and the Ontario Arts Council for our publishing program.

Typeset in Minion by M&S, Toronto
Printed and bound in Canada

This book is printed on acid-free paper that is 100% recycled, ancient-forest friendly (100% post-consumer recycled).

McClelland & Stewart Ltd.
The Canadian Publishers
481 University Avenue
Toronto, Ontario
M5G 2E9
www.mcclelland.com

1 2 3 4 5   09 08 07 06 05

Contents

Preface

Writing this book has been a pleasure for us both – despite the deadlines and long hours. In the process, we have become better grandmothers and better friends. We laughed and cried in our interviews and discussion groups with other grandparents, grandchildren, and young parents. We learned a lot from our review of the literature on grandparenting and child development. Our goal is to share some of what we have learned with you, the reader.

We met in our twenties when we were pregnant with our first children, and have remained best friends since then. Over the years, we bragged, agonized, commiserated, and rejoiced over how our children were getting on, and how we were doing as parents. Parenting was important to us. We read books, talked with other parents, and went to parenting classes. We were "intentional" parents who tried to think ahead about how best to handle the challenges and joys of parenting. This included our times as single parents, joint parents, and step-parents.

Now, each of us has four grown-up children in blended families with our second husbands. Together, we have fourteen grandchildren and are anticipating more. While loving our grandchildren is the most natural thing on earth, the grandparenting role is more complex than it used to be. There are multiple families in diverse relationships. Some of our children and grandchildren live thousands of miles and two time zones away. Unlike our own grandmothers, we are both still employed full-time. Logistics are complicated. Our children are older, more knowledgeable parents than we were. Birthing and child rearing have changed since our days with Dr. Spock and Parent Effectiveness Training.

We realized that if we were to be effective grandparents we would have to be intentional about how we did it, just as we were as parents. We scoured bookstores and the Internet, and came up with several good how-to books and Web sites that offer advice on everything from discipline to communication, and activities you can do with your grandchildren. We found only one book specifically aimed at the boomer generation, and very few that concentrated on some basic principles, rather than providing specific advice. The more we talked with grandparents and looked at the complexities of families today, the more we realized that flexibility and common sense combined with some basic child-centred principles were what we, and other grand-parents, needed most.

We hope that this book will inspire you to be an intentional and involved grandparent. Grandparenting is one of life's greatest sources of joy, fun, love, and satisfaction. And there is no doubt that you are an essential person in the lives of your grandchildren and their parents. Enjoy!

P.S. Peggy and Mary Jane would love to hear about your experience as a grandboomer and any comments you have about this book. Please contact us at: grandma@aldergroup.com.

Acknowledgements

We would like to thank all the grandparents, parents, and grandchildren who participated in our interviews and discussion groups, and who filled out our questionnaire. Your honesty and enthusiasm were inspiring and your stories are the best part of this book.

Thank you to Elizabeth Kribs, our excellent editor, who sharpened our prose and believes in the power of grandparenting. A number of people reviewed our work and provided valuable insight and feedback. We are especially grateful to Dr. Miroslava Lhotsky, Dr. Judy Turner, Dr. Joan Whitfield, and Susan Swanson. To our many other friends who gave us ideas and loving encouragement, thank you!

We'd also like to thank our wonderful children and their life partners: Lisa and Gord, Patty and Bob, Julie and Bradley, Portia and Eric, Jason and Jen, and Matthew and Nancy for providing us with grandchildren, and to acknowledge them for their intentional parenting skills. You make us want to be better grandparents. Danny and Kristin, Brendan and Valerie – no pressure, but we do look forward to additional grandchildren.

The inspiration for this book came from our fourteen delightful grandchildren – Ben, Andrew, Travis, Jordan, Nicholas, Haley, Cooper, Samuel, Alexa, Torin, Teia, Connor, Liam, and Emma. You light up our lives and fill us with joy.

And finally, we would like to pay special tribute to our husbands, Jo and Michael. Not only did they spend hours reviewing the manuscript and making us delicious meals, they are also wonderful, committed grandfathers who delight in their role.

We dedicate this book to grandparents and grandchildren everywhere. Doris and Lois, you are great-grandmothers extraordinaire. Grandpa Ted and Grandpa Seamus, we miss you dearly.

Peggy and Mary Jane

Intentional Grandparenting

Introduction

No cowboy was ever faster on the draw than a grandparent pulling a baby picture out of a wallet.

— Author Unknown

Congratulations! You are a grandparent or about to become one. Grandparenting is one of the greatest joys in life. We should know. Between us we have fourteen perfect grandchildren, and are looking forward to more.

Grandparents get to be heroes just for removing a splinter, playing hide-and-seek, filling a wading pool, or treating a losing baseball player like a winner (ice cream included). You get another chance to witness the first step, first word, first date, and first time behind the wheel. You can give and get more unconditional love than your heart can ever hold. Grandchildren are eager partners for blowing bubbles, flying kites, giggling, and reading the adventures of Pooh. You can add another branch to your family tree, and if you are lucky, there will be a long list in your obituary called "loving grandchildren and great grandchildren."

But wait a minute. You are also a boomer – part of that huge generation born between 1946 and 1964. Our anthem was Bob Dylan's "Forever Young." We vowed to "never trust anyone over age thirty." How did we become old enough to be grandparents?

Most boomers do a double take when they get the phone call from their son or daughter who breathlessly announces: "We're pregnant."

There is a rush of joy and excitement mixed with some niggling concerns in the back of their heads: "Do I have time to be a grandparent?" "I don't look or feel like a grandparent . . . I don't have grey hair or even wear glasses (thanks to hair dye and laser surgery). Am I really that old?"

Well, get ready. You are not the only one old enough to be a grandparent. The average age for first-time grandparents is forty-eight. In North America a boomer turns fifty every four seconds. By age sixty, about 75 per cent of boomers will have grandchildren. So do the math – by the year 2010 a grandparent will be "born" approximately every three seconds in North America. Marketers who anticipate the wave of toys and trips that boomers will buy for their grandchildren have already coined a name for the next stage of life for the Big Generation – "grandboomers."

THIS BOOK IS FOR YOU
This book is for boomer grandparents and grandboomers-to-be. We also hope that young parents will appreciate this book, give it to their parents, and discuss the parts that have meaning for them.

We believe that step-grandparents have the same responsibilities and roles, and deserve the same joys, as those who become grandparents through their own offspring. This was supported over and over by the men and women we interviewed. In almost all cases, being a "step" made no difference to the powerful feelings both grandmothers and grandfathers have for their grandchildren. Indeed, even the official U.S. and Canadian bureaus of statistics make no distinction between biological and step-grandparents when they collect information on grandparents today.

We would also like to acknowledge the millions of aunts, uncles, and other adults who play a grandparenting-type role in children's lives. The principles we describe can be equally effective for other adults who provide children with ongoing support and unconditional love. Like grandparents, these special people can make a huge difference in the lives of children and adolescents, and how they grow and develop into adulthood.

Some of you may be reluctant grandparents. It may seem too soon since your own children left home or you may feel overwhelmed with other commitments, such as a demanding job and caring for aging parents. It is okay to feel this way. But regardless of your readiness to get fully involved at this point, it still helps to think about the ten principles and many practical suggestions explored in this book. You are important to your adult children and their children, by the very nature of being a GRANDparent. With some planning and commitment you can make it a grand role, in a way that suits you and your current situation.

Some grandparents live alone with their grandchildren (without the parents) in what is called a "skip generation" household. In Canada, less than 1 per cent of children and adolescents are raised alone by their grandparents. In the United States, this number is significantly higher. Well over two million grandparents are raising one or more of their grandchildren on their own. While we hope this book will be helpful to those special grandparents who have taken on the parenting role, it does not specifically address their challenges. Fortunately, many of the Web sites we recommend in the Appendix provide additional information and support for grandparents who are parenting full-time.

Grandfathers Are Equally Important

In preparing to write this book we found a lot of material addressed to grandmothers. No wonder. In most cultures, women are more likely to be involved with young children than men, and grandmothers are the thread that holds generations together.

We believe that this generation of grandfathers will stand these traditions on their head. In the Healthy Boomer Midlife Survey carried out by Peggy and her co-authors for *The Healthy Boomer* and *The Juggling Act*, midlife men expressed a sincere desire to be more involved with their children and grandchildren than in the past. A recent survey by the American Association of Retired Persons (AARP) with their grandparent members showed that grandfathers were equally as likely as grandmothers to have dinner, watch movies or TV, go shopping with, and read to their grandchildren. Grandfathers participated in exercise and sports with their grandchildren much more often than grandmothers. Even at age eighty-plus, some 67 per cent of grandfathers reported playing active games and sports with their grandchildren in the past six months!

Our interviews with grandfathers confirmed these findings. Whether they were retired or working, the men we spoke with were enthusiastic and involved grandparents. Some suggested that increased involvement by grandfathers was a natural evolution, as our expectations for involved fathering have increased over the last thirty years. In one discussion group, Laird, a grandfather of two, summed it up when he said, "I never had time to really see and enjoy each stage of development with my own children. It's different with my grandchildren, and I love it."

EFFECTIVE GRANDPARENTING

What is effective grandparenting? We looked at studies and talked with the experts and other grandboomers. We asked young parents what they most appreciated and wanted from their parents as grandparents.

We also spoke with grandchildren ranging in age from six to sixteen about what they believed was an ideal grandfather or grandmother. Their candour and often humorous responses made us laugh out loud and gave us pause. One eight-year-old girl told us: "The ideal Grandpa is never grumpy. He has time to do things just with me. Things like fishing and soccer and cooking and playing Nintendo and going to the water park." This granddaughter was clearly tapping into the energy and fun that many grandboomers bring to their new role.

Ultimately it is you, after talking with your adult children, who need to decide the kind of grandparent you can and want to be. It is you who will decide what "ideal" means in your circumstances.

Grandparents and parents may sometimes disagree about the specifics of child rearing but on one thing there is no disagreement – we all want the best for our grandchildren. We want them to be happy, healthy, resilient, responsible, and competent. We want them to get along with others and to grow up making a contribution to their families and their world. We want them to have a strong sense of self-worth. We want them to feel special and appreciated.

Grandparents know a lot about how to help children grow up this way. After all, most of us have been through it with our children. We have acquired some wisdom over the years. Much of the way you grandparent will be based on your knowledge, intuition, and experience. At the same time, it is helpful to have a set of guidelines to reflect on, especially when we consider the changes in families, work, and school since we were parents.

THE TIMES, THEY ARE A CHANGING

Some grandboomers have wonderful memories of their own grandparents and the love and support they received from them. Others are not so lucky. As the children of immigrants, many of us never knew or hardly saw our grandparents. In many cases, our grandparents died during the war or from an illness that medicine was less able to treat back then. We live in a very different world today.

Happily, grandparents are living longer. This means that four- and even five-generation families are becoming more common. It also means that most boomers find themselves in the sandwich generation, helping with aging parents and grandchildren at the same time. Some, like forty-eight-year-old Doreen who became a grandmother two years ago, and still has a sixteen-year-old son at home, are part of the "club sandwich" generation.

In addition to living longer, more older adults are living disability-free than in our parents' generation. This means that, in general, grandboomers look and feel young. They bring a different style to the traditional role: wearing jeans, riding their bikes, and playing street hockey with their grandchildren.

In the 1940s, '50s, and '60s, it was extremely rare for grandmothers to be working outside the home. Today, because of the huge influx of boomer women into the workforce after the 1960s, many midlife grandmothers are still employed (and short on time to babysit and bake cookies). On the other hand, many boomer men born in the mid- to late forties are retiring before age sixty-five, and now have more time for grandparenting at an earlier age than their fathers did.

Parenting, like grandparenting, has changed too. There are new theories and modes of child rearing. Babies are being birthed under- water and new mothers collect and store their breast milk so they can return to work and still breast-feed. The economic, technological, social, and school environments our children grew up in have all sub- stantially changed. Kids learn algebra in public school, preteens carry cellphones, and young drivers must pass through a "graduated system" of licences to prove they are safe on the road. As grandparents, we need to get in tune with life in the modern family.

Throughout this book, you will find selected research statistics and references to "Then and Now," which describe some of the differences between our lives as kids and life for children and families in the twenty- first century. Some of the changes – such as the trend for more young people to get a college or university education – are very positive. But many of the changes suggest that North American society is less family- friendly than when we or our children were growing up. Modern fami- lies face challenges related to time, money, and family dynamics. Consider these facts, taken from Canadian and U.S. census data:

- About 70 per cent of families with young children have two wage-earning parents. As a result, children have less time with their parents. One American study showed that today's parents spend an average of ten to twelve fewer waking hours per week with their children than parents did thirty years ago.

- The option of one parent staying home to provide childcare is unrealistic for most families. Employment insecurity, the cost of housing, and economic conditions are such that if one parent in every family stayed home, the number of poor children in Canada would double to almost three million. In the U.S. in 2002, 10 per cent of full-time working families with children were still poor (annual income that is below the poverty level of $15,000), despite the fact that one or both parents had jobs.

- In the 1940s and '50s, a child's chance of growing up with both parents was 80 per cent. Today, because of relationship and marriage breakdowns, it is less than 50 per cent, in both Canada and the U.S.

- Growing rates of marriage and common-law relationship breakdowns and remarriage may decrease or sever grandparents' access to their grandchildren. This has led to increased calls to protect the rights of grandparents and grandchildren to see each other, in both the United States and Canada.

- Modern families are increasingly diverse. The number of single-parent families and biracial and intercultural unions, as well as foreign adoptions is increasing. Same-sex unions are more common and same-sex marriages are now legal in several provinces in Canada. In many cases, diverse families still face discrimination and legal sanctions that fail to embrace the positive strengths these families bring to North American society.

The point of comparing the past and present is not to suggest that we must return to "the good old days" or even to suggest that those days were better. It is to show us that we must recognize and respond to today's challenges. The traditional family many of us grew up in – Dad, Mom-at-home, four children, and Grampa all living together until death do us part – is (almost) no more. For example, each of Mary Jane and Peggy's grandchildren has three or four sets of grandparents and multiple great-grandparents; all have more aunts, uncles, and cousins than we can count. Our blended, extended families live all over Canada, the United States, and other parts of the world.

Yet, the family remains the foundation of our society and the core of our personal happiness. Grandparents who provide stable connections and unconditional love are needed more than ever.

WHAT MAKES GRANDBOOMERS UNIQUE?

As we looked at the research on grandparenting and the growing number of books on the subject, the name Arthur Kornhaber kept coming up. Dr. Kornhaber, who is sometimes called "the guru" of grandparenting, is the founder of the Foundation for Grandparenting. His impressive grandparenting study began in the seventies and continues to this day. Some of his initial findings, which were published in 1981 in *Grandparents/Grandchildren: The Vital Connection*, included the following:

- The grandparent-grandchild bond is second in importance only to the parent-child bond.
- Grandparents and grandchildren deeply affect each other's lives.
- Parents and grandchildren benefit greatly when grandparents are involved with their families.
- Grandparenting provides many seniors with meaning and joy.

While we are convinced that these fundamental findings remain true today, many things have changed in the environment of the twenty-first century. The 2002 Grandparenting Survey carried out by the American Association of Retired Persons (AARP) was the first study to look at grandboomers (born between 1946 and 1964). The majority (69 per cent) are employed, and five in ten have attended or graduated from college.

Not surprisingly, many of the differences between grandboomers and non-boomer grandparents relate to the age of both the grandparents and the grandchildren. Grandboomers (who are younger) are more likely to participate in physical activities with their grandchildren, while non-boomers are more likely to help their grandchildren (who are older) with school work. While both sets of grandparents spend similar amounts of money on their grandchildren, grandboomers report spending a much higher percentage than non-boomers on necessities, such as living expenses (57 per cent versus 42 per cent) and medical/ dental costs (31 per cent versus 23 per cent).

A CHILD DEVELOPMENT APPROACH

While each child develops and grows at their own pace, there are some general and specific stages that children and adolescents go through in terms of their physical, intellectual, social, and emotional development. In the last twenty to thirty years, there has been an impressive acceleration in the research related to child development, particularly in our understanding of early brain development and the first six years of life. Other studies have revealed much about the factors that help children make a positive transition into adolescence and adulthood.

You will find many books and resources describing what to expect at each stage; for example, the age at which most children begin to sit, crawl, stand, and walk. We encourage you to look at this kind of material so that you can anticipate and share each of these marvellous developments with your grandchildren's parents. We do not intend to duplicate this kind of information here.

Rather, our goal in this book is to step back and reflect on how some of the new findings related to healthy child development influence each of the ten principles and how we put them into practice.

There are at least three good reasons for using a child development approach. First, it will help us understand what is most important, and how we can be most supportive at different stages of our grandchildren's development. Secondly, it will help us have realistic expectations and be better prepared to play with and care for our grandchildren in ways that are both physically and emotionally safe. Lastly, we will understand what our adult children are talking about when they discuss terms and phrases like "attachment," "neuron synapses," and "responding to cues."

TEN PRINCIPLES

This book presents ten basic but powerful principles that can enrich your experience as a grandparent, while giving your grandchildren and their parents the support, respect, nurturing, and love they need.

Ten Principles for Effective Grandparenting
1. Determine the kind of grandparent you want to be.
2. Respect and support the parents.
3. Be open to new possibilities.
4. Embrace diversity.
5. Be accepting, empathetic, and positive.
6. Be playful and spontaneous.
7. Be consistent, reliable, and fair.
8. Stay in touch.
9. Be organized but flexible.
10. Take care of you.

As our selection of principles evolved we realized that some important issues and practices, such as distance and open communication, cut across all of the principles. In the end, we asked parents and grandparents to validate the ten principles and they said they were comprehensive and helpful.

Everyone agreed that each of the ten principles was important in its own right. But no matter how basic or important a principle is, applying it day after day is not always easy. That is why each chapter contains questions and answers and real-life stories about how others put the principles into practice. These stories may not be directly applicable in your situation, but they will help you reflect on how you might design your strategies for intentional grandparenting.

THE LAST WORD

As you will find in the chapters that follow, we like to give the last word to grandchildren or to humorous anecdotes sent to us by other grandparents and parents. Here are some of the things children ages seven to ten told us about grandmothers and grandfathers:

The world's greatest grandmother . . .

- Likes to go fishing and makes a lot of good food;
- Cuddles with me and has me for sleepovers;
- Likes pizza and hanging out the clothes;
- Is nice, rich, and works in a candy shop.

The world's greatest grandfather . . .

- Is nice, old, tall, and fun (*wow!*);
- Plays with me and takes me everywhere;
- Calls me "Twinker";
- Climbs trees with me and gives me money.

If I could change one thing about my grandmother . . .

- She'd let me stay up later;
- She'd stop pinching my cheeks;
- She would take us swimming more, and help us build things;
- She and my Granddad would live together;
- I would not change anything; I love her the way she is (*multiple responses*).

If I could change one thing about my grandfather . . .

- He would do more things with me;
- We would *not* go fishing;

- He would give me more kisses;
- He would not get older;
- He would get me a cat;
- I would not change anything; I love him the way he is (*multiple responses*).

Determine the Kind of Grandparent You Want to Be

If you don't know where you are going, any road will do.
— Inspired by Lewis Carroll, *Alice in Wonderland*

Last year, Maureen attended a memorial service for her friend Richard's mother. The deceased was the wife of a very successful businessman, the mother of four accomplished sons, and a grandmother of nine. After Richard had spoken eloquently about her, his brother read aloud a letter from his daughter, Sonia, who couldn't attend. Maureen describes her reaction to the letter:

> Sonia talked about how strong an influence her grandmother had been, despite the generation gap and the very traditional role her grandmother had played. She described her generosity, her integrity, her varied interests and most specifically, how she had been such a supporting presence in all her grandchildren's lives. Everyone was so moved by this loving letter. I knew then that I wanted my grandchildren to write such a tribute to me when I died.

The first principle of grandparenting is the springboard for your role as a grandparent: determine the kind of grandparent you want to be. If your grandchildren were to write your eulogy, what would you want them to say? Would it be about what you have accomplished? How you helped them? Inspired them? Amused them? Played with them? Loved them? How you built a tree house together? Taught them to fish? How you were always gentle or full of energy?

Mary Jane explains how she felt when her granddaughter Alexa, who was almost six, described her as the grandma "who always laughs and gives big hugs."

> While this was a fairly accurate picture, I also wanted her to remember me as the grandma who spent time with her, who listened to her, who taught her things. The more I thought about it, the more I realized that I could not leave this to happenstance. I needed to develop a clear picture of the kind of grandparent I wanted to be and what that meant in terms of committing my time and energy. I needed to create a personal vision and strategy for grandparenting.

In this chapter you will discover a process for developing your vision for grandparenting and identify strategies for making it happen. We refer to this process as "intentional grandparenting" – planning ahead and taking deliberate action to be the kind of grandparent you want to be.

In her book *The Essential Grandparent*, Lillian Carson, a psychotherapist and grandmother, talks about the importance of planning our role as a grandparent. Her work as a therapist has confirmed the notion that neither parenting nor grandparenting are instinctual. We need to clarify our intentions as a grandparent and then develop some strategies to get us there. The grandparent role has the potential to enrich our lives and those of our children and grandchildren, or to cause stress and discord. A little thought and effort can make the difference in how our role plays out.

THEN AND NOW
Our grandparents might have laughed at the notion of applying strategic planning concepts to grandparenting. Isn't grandparenting just another form of parenting, but without all that responsibility? And

don't both just come naturally? Our generation knows all too well that it is more complicated than this. Modern grandparents must adjust to blended families, step-grandparenting, distance, and other changes in family structures. Today's standards for parenting are higher and more explicit than when we were parents. Our children have access to research and theories on a myriad of topics, ranging from how to stimulate the neonatal infant to how to manage your child's sleeping habits. While this is helpful, it can be confusing as well.

Social expectations of us as grandparents are also greater and more complex. Most of our children assume that we will be involved and active grandparents, but they don't necessarily assume that we have all the answers. Many are better educated than we were as parents. Now, there are over two thousand titles on child rearing available; then, we had Dr. Spock. Linda, a grandmother of three, describes it this way:

> I shouldn't have been surprised when my daughter-in-law informed me that because child rearing had changed so much, she and her friends relied on each other for advice and information, not their parents. Clearly I was valued as a grandparent, but not as someone she would turn to for advice on how to get my grandson to eat broccoli. Getting your children to eat vegetables is somehow much more complicated than when we were parents. There are whole books devoted to the subject. Dr. Spock covered vegetables in three lines.

In addition to higher expectations, we grandparents have more complex lives. We are busy: many of us are still working and we may have more interests and hobbies than our grandparents did. Likely we travel more and have more disposable income. We are preoccupied. We schedule time with our grandchildren in our daily planners.

CRAFTING YOUR VISION

We all have an image of the ideal grandparent, shaped by our own experiences and values. It was clear from our interviews that while most grandboomers had spent little time in conscious reflection, their actions implied definitive values and principles underlying how they grandparent.

Myrna, who is a busy senior executive and an involved grandmother with ten grandchildren, was typical in the way she responded to a question about her vision of grandparenting.

> I've never really given it much thought. But I guess if I think about it now, I want to share my values and my perspective on life with my grandchildren. I want each of them to feel special and to know that they have somewhere to go, no matter what. I want to be there for them and give them my time.

Myrna then went on to describe the evolution of her grandparenting style from an activity-focused grandparent (wanting to do things with the grandchildren) to a confidence-building grandparent (wanting to help the grandchildren feel good about themselves).

Whether we have articulated it or not, most of us have a vision and a philosophy of grandparenting. The question we might ask ourselves is this: are we being thoughtful and intentional in our behaviours or would we do things differently if we spent a little more time in reflection?

Grandparenting is an important aspect of family life and there is value in reflecting on our role up front. For those of you who are new or soon-to-be grandparents, this is an opportunity to start off on the right foot, confident that you have an understanding of your hopes and dreams as a grandparent. With a clearer vision of the future, your actions are more likely to support your intentions. For those of us that are veteran grandparents, confirming our long-term goals will help us see what changes we need to make to ensure we are being the grandparents we want to be. Steven Covey, author of *The 7 Habits of Highly Effective Families*, compares having a vision or mission to having a destination and a compass – necessary items for any journey.

This section includes a series of questions and suggested exercises to help you develop a personal vision of the kind of grandparent you want to be. This process has four steps:

1. Reflect on your own experiences as a grandchild and how they have shaped you.
2. Think about your stand on some of the key aspects of grandparenting.
3. Consult with your adult children during the process.
4. Describe your vision.

Step 1: Reflect on your own experiences as a grandchild and how they have shaped you.
Think back to when you were a grandchild. How involved were your grandparents in your life? How did they make you feel? What did they do to demonstrate that they loved you and that you were special? What did they do that made you feel sad, unloved, or inadequate? What are your favourite memories? When you think of your grandmother, what images come to mind? When you think of your grandfather, what images come to mind?

From our interviews and research we know that there is little common ground here; our experiences are as varied as snowflakes. For some of us, our grandparents were central to our lives and brought stability and hope. Audrey, a grandmother of five, talks about the loving relationship she had with her grandfather.

> I had a wonderful granddad and I spent a lot of time with him. My memories of him are very important for me. Granddad showed me how to be a person of your word. I learned to really like and respect other people. I spent a lot of time alone with him on his farm and we would walk for miles in his garden. He was great at chatter and he made me feel loved and secure.

For others, grandparents were either difficult or a nonentity. Anne, a twenty-five-year-old mother, describes her situation.

> My grandparents were grumpy and anxious, especially my grand-mother. I hated how they treated my mom and us kids. We couldn't sit on any of the good furniture and everything was too much effort, so they seldom even made us a meal. We tried to pretend we had a relationship, but we didn't and it made us all sad. They both died a few years ago. We now realize that my grandmother was mentally ill and that Grandpa just tried to please her. The irony is that they were so miserly with their time and money, but left us a fair amount of money when they died. How sad. It would have been so much better to have had their love and affection when they were alive.

Our challenge is to understand how our experience has influenced us, and determine if our relationship with our own grandparents has enhanced or limited our own possibilities. Should I spend my time baking cookies because that is how my grandmother showed me love and affection? Will this give me pleasure and satisfaction? Is this what my grandchildren need? Is it the best way to support their parents?

Grandparents can be more effective by considering things from their children and grandchildren's points of view, rather than just reacting without thinking. Winnie describes how this approach has changed the way she bakes:

> I have learned that it is more fun to bake cookies *with* my young grandchildren, than *for* them. They each have their own apron and small oven mitts (although I have yet to let them near the oven!). The baking includes a lesson in hygiene: they have to wash their hands before coming near the ingredients. For me, it is a lesson in patience, making sure all are involved equally in the process, despite the age differences. For the grandchildren, the highlight is eating the batter. I should say, *used* to be eating the batter. Their

mother recently brought to my attention that the raw eggs in batter are potentially harmful to children, so now we all focus on the finished product.

Step 2: Think about your stand on some of the key aspects of grandparenting.

Developing clarity around your role will increase your enjoyment and satisfaction as a grandparent, and probably that of your grandchildren and adult children as well. There are a number of practical questions to consider. Where two grandparents are involved, we suggest you discuss the following issues as a couple.

How often do you want to see your grandchildren? What changes will this involve?

For our friend, Peggy R., this was an easy decision. Close to retirement, with her daughter living nearby, Peggy was clear that she wanted to see her daughter and granddaughters as often as she could. She made herself available on an almost daily basis, either as an occasional babysitter, or as a drop-in centre for tea, cookies, advice, and admiration. This was a conscious decision that required her to put her consulting and mediation practice temporarily on hold. Peggy says: "I did so happily, knowing that being with my grandchildren and supporting my daughter as a new parent would bring me far more pleasure than working at my job."

Many grandparents are not as fortunate. Our grandchildren may live in a different city or country and our children may be unable or unwilling to bring them to visit us. We may not have a close relationship with our adult children or in-laws. We may have limited income or be unable to travel for health reasons. Despite all of these factors, the majority of grandparents make a special effort to spend time with their children and grandchildren.

When their daughter Samantha married an Orthodox rabbi and moved from Canada to Israel, Marcy and Tony sat down as a couple to develop a strategy. They were determined that distance was not going to be an obstacle to a close and loving relationship with Samantha, her husband, and their grandchildren. Marcy talks about the decisions they made.

> We decided to see our grandchildren face-to-face at least twice a year for an extended period of time, and to find creative ways to stay in touch in between. This vision meant that we had to make some changes in our lifestyle. We downsized our home, delayed Tony's retirement date, planned our vacations around trips to Israel, and scheduled our family events to coincide with Samantha's trips to Canada. We are happy with our choices and very close to our four granddaughters, despite the distance.

For many of us, putting our career plans on hold, or travelling across the world to visit our children and grandchildren for a month is not an option. Nor is every grandparent necessarily interested in spending a lot of time with his or her grandchildren. Your challenge is to think ahead about how much time you want and are able to spend with your grandchildren, given your unique situation. Then you need to identify the changes in your schedule and lifestyle this will involve.

What traditions do you want to establish with your grandchildren?
Grandparents are in the business of creating happy childhood memories. Happy memories and a sense of identity are built through traditions and shared activities. It is never too early to decide what activities, hobbies, and cultural traditions you would like to engage in with your grandchildren. Will it be storytelling, baking, fishing, playing sports, playing board games, going to the library, going to the movies, or having time-honoured meals on special days? Many of these traditions will arise spontaneously as you get to know and interact with your grandchildren. But how much better if some of them intentionally flow from your values and the kind of activities that bring you and your grandchildren joy?

Bonnie and Dick are keen environmentalists. They combine their love of travel with their interests in birdwatching and their intent to preserve the planet's natural resources. They travel mainly on foot or by bike. They stay in senior hostels and often volunteer for short environmental projects in the countries they visit. Bonnie describes how these values are the basis for the traditions they are establishing with their grandson, Connor.

> We love to take Connor for long nature walks and skating on the canal in the winter. He has been on the train to Kingston to visit his great-grandparents' farm. Last week his other grandmother told me that Connor pointed out a red bird to her and told her it was a cardinal. She thought it was a robin. Connor is only three years old.

What important family values do you want to encourage in your grandchildren? How will you do this?
What were the family values that were important to you when you raised your children? Looking back, what would you do differently? What values would you stress now? How do these differ from your adult children's values? How do you see your role in terms of imparting values to your grandchildren? How would you encourage your values, while respecting your adult children in their role as parents? While all the research supports the notion that example is the best teacher, is there anything else you can do to encourage your grandchildren to adopt the values that have been passed down as part of your heritage?

Sally, whose son-in-law has been arrested for petty theft, makes a point of modelling honesty, which is an integral value in her life.

> We read books that have honesty as a theme, and I look for opportunities to show my grandkids what honesty looks like in daily interactions. I know that all kids lie from time to time, but I address it in an open and loving way when they tell lies. I always acknowledge and reward them when I "catch them" being honest.

What is your policy on babysitting?
Babysitting gives us a wonderful opportunity to get to know our grandchildren on a whole new level. We can be ourselves. We have our grandchildren's undivided attention and more importantly, they have ours. It is also an opportunity to support your adult children in their busy and complicated lives.

But minding children is not everyone's cup of tea. We need to sort out our feelings early on in our role as a grandparent. Do I want to babysit my grandchildren? How often? Am I willing to give up my weekends to babysit? How much am I willing to be inconvenienced? Will I insist that my grandchildren come to my home where I can also carry on some of my day-to-day activities, or am I willing to go to their home? What changes do I need to make in my life if I decide to be an occasional babysitter? What changes do I need to make to my home? How much am I able and willing to do to make it easier for the parents when I babysit? Will I buy cribs and high chairs and toys and books and diapers so they don't have to drag all their baby paraphernalia with them to my home every time they visit? How comfortable am I if an emergency should arise?

Audrey is a manager in her late fifties, divorced with six grandchildren, two of whom live in the same city. Previously her daughter and two young grandchildren lived with her for a few years. Audrey is very clear about her role as a babysitter for her grandchildren. She doesn't want to be one.

> I frequently take my grandchildren for the weekend, but I don't consider this babysitting. The visits are on my terms and happen at my convenience. I support my children in their role as parents, but I don't want them to be dependent on me to babysit. I want the freedom to choose. I like to help but I don't want to feel that I have to.

For Dick and Jane, (yes, these really are their real names, and they have a dog called Fish), babysitting is a key strategy for getting to know their grandchildren. They live in Ottawa, Ontario, and their daughter Catherine and her family live in New Jersey. Offering to babysit for an extended period of time at least three times a year works well for now, but Dick recognizes that it may be more difficult in the future.

> We welcome the opportunity to mind our two young grand-children three or four times a year. Now that we have both just retired, it is not difficult to manage our schedule around Catherine's needs, despite our active and busy lifestyle. But we have three other adult children, who are not yet married. We wonder how we will manage to provide the same level of support when and if there are four sets of grandchildren. Our other children have already raised this. They encourage us to stay healthy and hope we will have the same energy for our future grandchildren.

Deciding up front doesn't mean that our decisions are cast in stone or that we can't change our minds. It is much easier and less disruptive, however, to become more willing to babysit than to become resentful or retreat because we have overcommitted ourselves.

What about gift-giving and spending on your grandchildren?
According to a large survey carried out by the American Association of Retired Persons, the average grandboomer in the U.S. spends between $250 and $500 a year on each grandchild. This is not an inconsequential amount considering the average grandparent has six grandchildren. Decisions around spending on our grandchildren can be complex. Will your spending strategy be more long-term or short-term (e.g., school funds versus toys)? What impact will the other grandparents' spending philosophy have on your spending? Do you need to spend the same amount on each grandchild or does it depend on their needs? What

about step-grandchildren? What do your adult children expect and want from you in terms of gifts and financial support for their children?

Kathleen wishes she had given more thought to her gift-giving approach up front. When her first grandchild arrived, she enthusiastically purchased expensive designer clothes, books, and toys, most often without consulting her stepdaughter. Kathleen describes how she has changed. She now stops before she shops!

> The books I bought proved perfect but the clothes were seldom worn and the toys were often in poor repair by the time my granddaughter was old enough to play with them. By the advent of my third grandchild, I had a much more effective gift-giving strategy. I consulted the parents and my grandchildren first about what was wanted and needed. I followed the lead of the other grandparents, and began to give a small present and a contribution toward my grandchildren's educations on their birthdays.

What is your approach regarding the other grandparents?
Because of separation and divorce, many of us will share the grandparenting role with numerous other grandparents. We may be asked ahead of time what we want to be called by our grandchildren so that we are all uniquely identified. Given the differences that we will all have in our approaches to grandparenting, this is probably not necessary. Our grandchildren will soon begin to sort us out. What we need to think about is the kind of relationship we would like to have with the other grandparents and how we will handle our differences.

The grandboomers we interviewed were fairly consistent in their approach to other grandparents. While some did have philosophical differences with the other grandparents, their first concerns were the needs and feelings of their adult children and grandchildren. Putting this philosophy into practice isn't always easy.

Diana and Alex describe how frustrating it was at first to deal with their son-in-law's parents. Dubbed the "designer grandparents" by

Diana, they would fly in to visit their new grandchild with gifts and much fanfare, only to stay a day and leave. Despite the copious photos in their home of the new grandchild, these grandparents were uninterested in spending time with the grandchildren. She talked incessantly about how difficult childbirth was for her and how she never really liked babies. He talked about all the things he would do with his grandson once he was old enough, whatever age that might be.

> We held back at the beginning because we did not want to exaggerate the differences, and make our son-in-law feel bad. After a few months, however, we came to the conclusion that we had to go our own way – to be the engaged, enthusiastic, and involved grandparents we wanted to be. We were not responsible for their behaviour. Why should we and our grandson miss out?

Step 3: Consult with your adult children during the process.
Hindsight is always twenty-twenty. Writing this book has made both of us realize that we did not spend enough time early on consulting with our adult children to determine their expectations of us as grandparents. We made a number of assumptions based on our experiences as parents. Not only would these discussions have helped us be more effective and satisfied as grandparents, but they would also have helped our children clarify their feelings around our grandparenting practices.

Reflecting and consulting on your role as a grandparent early in the process allows you to be more intentional. Your feelings will of course evolve as you experience the wonderful stages of your grandchildren's development. By remaining open with their parents, you are more likely to find joy and satisfaction in your role.

Step 4: Describe your vision.
Research shows that we are much more likely to live a vision we have written down. Here are two techniques for crafting your vision as a grandparent.

1. Write your eulogy.

Draft a eulogy which focuses on your role as a grandparent. Here are some ideas of what to describe:

- The things you did with your grandchildren. Be specific.
- The values you taught them.
- The traditions and activities you enjoyed together.
- The things that made you both laugh.
- What they will miss most about you.
- How their lives were better because you were there.

2. Create a simple picture of the future.

Think about your life at seventy-five. Imagine that you are surrounded by your grandchildren and consider the following questions.

- Where are you living?
- What are you doing with your grandchildren?
- How often do you see them?
- What do you talk about?
- Whom do they bring along with them to see you?
- What are your favourite memories with them?
- What are you most proud of in terms of your relationship with them?
- What have they learned from you?
- What have you learned from them?
- What do they appreciate most about you?

WHAT GETS IN THE WAY OF INTENTIONAL GRANDPARENTING?

One assumption that we made in writing this book is that most grand-boomers are as interested in intentional grandparenting as we are, and sometimes just as perplexed by the challenges. For both of us, planning and strategizing are as natural as breathing – we are consultants after all. But for other grandparents, this way of operating may be as foreign as planning for retirement. Nice idea, but who has the time?

I am busier now than ever before

In some ways, being a busy grandparent may facilitate the determination of a vision for the kind of grandparent you want to be. Busy grandparents need to be strategic to ensure they spend their time wisely. They know that if they don't plan ahead – especially those with more than one set of grandchildren – weeks may go by without any contact with their grandchildren. Many grandparents handle this dilemma by planning for regular contact.

Maureen and Susan have one set of grandchildren over for dinner every Wednesday evening. The other grandchildren are younger and come over Thursday afternoon and often stay for dinner. Maureen describes how this works well for all:

> I work from home and since the children sleep in the afternoons for a few hours, I can often get some work done at the same time. Because the visits are regularly scheduled we can also plan activities ahead of time. We do weekly crafts with our grandchildren and we usually bake cookies or cakes together that they then take home to their parents. This schedule is sometimes interrupted but it allows everyone involved to try and plan around it.

I would rather be spontaneous

Being spontaneous is one of the most joyful aspects of grandparenting. On some issues, however, it helps to think about and decide on your stand ahead of time. What are your values around sharing? What are your rules for "keeping the house clean"? How much TV can grandchildren watch at your house? Will you treat all the grandchildren the same (e.g., bedtimes, sleepovers) or does age have its privileges? How will you handle discipline problems? By discussing these issues with family and getting clarity on your own position and intentions, you will be less likely to react without thinking when tricky situations arise.

Like parents, grandparents need to think through their philosophy and approach up front so that we aren't caught off-guard. There is more than a little truth in the expression: "If we don't have time to do it right the first time, we will need to find time to do it again." With a little thought and planning, grandparents can get it right the first time.

We were parents, this is easy

We sometimes make a number of assumptions as new grandparents. Our adult children will raise their children like we raised them. They will have similar values and priorities. They will face similar challenges and issues. They will turn to us for advice. We will love being a grandparent. Things will work out in the wash.

Many of these assumptions will prove to be false. Our children will incorporate some of our values and practices in their parenting, but not all. Their life partners will also come with a set of sometimes conflicting values and methods for child rearing. The environment in which we raised our children is quite different from today's and the situations we will face as grandparents will be different than those we faced as parents. There is a newly extended family to take into account. And most importantly, we are not the parents. Parents and grandparents have different roles. Just as it took time for us to learn how to parent, it will take time to learn how to be an effective grandparent.

QUESTIONS AND ANSWERS

Q: My son just remarried and I am a step-grandmother to two young boys aged six and eight. Can I have the same expectations as a real grandmother?

A: You are a real grandmother. It is up to you to decide what kind of grandparent you want to be and work towards that. The ten principles still apply. You do have the added challenge of first building a relationship with the grandchildren and of course their mother. This takes time but is usually easier when the grandchildren are younger. Principle Four: Embrace Diversity provides more information about step-grandparenting.

Q: My husband thinks being a grandparent is something that just happens naturally. How can I get him to think about grandparenting more strategically?

A: Once you are clear about your intentions as a grandparent, perhaps you could share this with him and ask him what he thinks. Hopefully, this will open up a discussion and you will discover where you think alike and where you differ. Be open to his opinions. Being judgmental about his intentions will probably only make him defensive. You may be surprised at the results.

WHAT THE RESEARCH TELLS US

Vision Is Key to Intentional Grandparenting

The importance of creating a vision that will drive your actions has been well documented in the fields of sport, psychology, and leadership development. According to Steven Covey, vision, more than any other factor, affects the choices we make and the way we spend our time. If our vision does not extend beyond what we are doing this week, then we tend to make choices based on what is directly in front of us. This is very limiting.

Source: Covey, S. *First Things First*. New York: Simon & Schuster, 1994.

The Importance of Self-Awareness

Reflecting on our role as a grandparent – our hopes, our dreams, our concerns, and our expectations – means being honest with ourselves about our feelings, good and bad. This reflection is called self-awareness. According to Daniel Goleman, the author of numerous books on emotional intelligence, self-awareness is essential for personal growth. If we hope to grow and evolve in our role as grandparents, we need to spend some time becoming more self-aware.

Source: Goleman, D. *Emotional Intelligence*. New York: Bantam Books, 1997.

Grandparents Make an Effort to See Their Grandchildren

According to a recent survey by the American Association of Retired Persons (AARP), over three-quarters of grandboomers saw their grandchildren between once a week and once a month, despite the fact that the majority (68 per cent) are still employed.

Source: American Association of Retired Persons (AARP). Grandparenting Survey, 2002. www.aarp.org/confacts/grandparents

THE LAST WORD

When Peggy R.'s father died, his eldest grandchild delivered one of the eulogies. Judd talked about what it was like to be with his grandfather.

He was not a special occasion grandfather. He was not someone we saw only at Christmas and Easter or spoke to over a long-distance line on our birthdays. He was there for me every day of the week, for thirty-three years. To recount memories of Grandpa would be to tell you the stories of our lives. So instead I have chosen to remind you of what it felt like to be with Harold, our grandfather.

- It was that time when you felt safe.
- The time when someone laughed louder than you did and the time when you were stunned by someone's overwhelming generosity.
- The time someone sat in the stands to watch you compete and cheered you on, and that brief moment when you actually believed the world revolved around you.
- It was that time you realized some people really do have perfect hair and perfect smiles, and the time you'd heard that story once too often.

- It was the time someone read a book to you, took you fishing, sang you a song, or bought you skates.
- The time someone inexplicably had a sailboat on their front lawn or painted their garage floor bright yellow.
- It was the time you saw a man who was so much more than he ever believed he was.

It would take me another thirty-three years to tell you how sad I am at this moment. So I'll finish by saying I recognize that men cannot be perfect. However, I do believe that certain special individuals are capable of doing something perfectly. And Harold was a perfect grandfather.

Respect and Support
the Parents

Everyone is entitled to my opinion.

– Yogi Berra

The temptation to provide our adult children with all the lessons learned from our many years of parenting is sometimes over-whelming. Why shouldn't they benefit from our successes and our mistakes? We could save them a lot of time, effort, and heartache. While they have probably absorbed many of our child-rearing philosophies and practices at a subconscious level, why not make these more explicit? Why not, indeed?

This chapter deals with one of the more challenging of the ten principles: Respect and support the parents of your grandchildren. Or, in the words of many of the grandboomers we interviewed, "zip your lips." Actually, a more accurate summary of this principle might be: if you can't say something positive, don't say anything at all. The exception to this rule is, of course, when the health or safety of a grandchild or parent is in jeopardy.

Respect and support are the underpinnings of all good relationships. In the context of this book, respect and support means being there emotionally and practically for your adult children and their partners, without being intrusive (synonyms: interfering, disturbing, invasive, meddling, and pushy). This principle is based on the assumption that our adult children and their partners are capable people who will learn and grow in their role as parents, just as we did. It is also based on our belief that one of the more important contributions we can make as grandparents is to provide support, empathy, and encouragement to the parents, not unsolicited advice – however well-intentioned. This does not mean that we shouldn't share our wisdom and experience, but rather that we need to do so in a way that honours the parents.

THEN AND NOW

From our conversations with young parents, it is clear that they want and need our support and involvement as grandparents, as much as we did as new parents. What is also clear is that we need to shake off the cobwebs of our own experiences and assumptions, and consider the environment in which our adult children are parenting. For the most part, this generation of new parents does not have to rely on the experience and advice of family members as much as we did.

In 1965, the average age of a first marriage was twenty-one for women and twenty-four for men. Now most couples decide to marry or live common-law in their late twenties and early thirties (U.S. and Canadian census data). Parents today are older and generally better educated than we were when we began to parent. Many modern mothers have had interesting and challenging careers before becoming a parent. They are used to making decisions and taking charge of their lives. They face motherhood with more confidence than our generation perhaps did. Many of us were learning how to parent and navigate the work world at the same time, and taking turns feeling inadequate at both.

Modern parents also come armed with research and theories that were unavailable to most of us grandboomers. Today's parent can access the most current research on any child-related topic on-line, faster than they can track down the modern grandboomer in her office or on the golf course.

While being informed is unquestionably a good thing, there is a downside to the intensity that many modern parents bring to their role, especially with their first child. Joan Whitfield, an experienced pediatrician, talks about this:

> Many parents now do it by the book. Our society has set up unreal expectations. They had to do well in school and in their careers; now they believe they must be perfect parents. They demand a lot of themselves. I always remind new parents that it's important to relax and just have fun with your kids.

Another major difference is the involvement of young fathers before, during, and after the birth. Peggy tells the story of her son-in-law Bradley, who read every child development book he could get his hands on when his wife, Julie, became pregnant. At the birth of his son, he explained to Peggy that he had synthesized the information on bonding with newborns into two key practices: he would read to his son every day, and take Sam into the bath with him every evening. His enthusiasm for parenting prompted Peggy to suggest that in his next life, he might want to come back as a sea horse, the only species where the male gives birth to the young.

Being well-informed and actively involved is the norm, not the exception for today's fathers. For our generation, child rearing was largely considered the mother's domain, regardless of whether she worked outside the home. Our partners may have participated keenly in child rearing, but it would be the rare boomer husband who debated the merits of various toilet-training techniques with his wife. Today, many of our sons and sons-in-law are as well-informed and competent in all aspects of child rearing as their life partners. The roles are often interchangeable, with the exception of breast-feeding, much to the disappointment of many a new mother with cracked nipples.

The result is that, sadly, we grandboomers are not always considered the indispensable sages that many of us would like to be. Our challenge is to find a way to bring our experience and wisdom to the table, while respecting our adult children and their partners in their role as parents. This chapter explores various ways to make that happen, but first, let's look at the rationale behind this principle.

DEMONSTRATING RESPECT AND SUPPORT

Showing respect and support for the parents of our grandchildren is an overriding principle that should drive many of the choices and decisions we make as grandparents. Not all our adult children and their partners are at the same level in terms of maturity, competence, and capacity for parenting. Nonetheless, grandparents need to apply this principle in a way that makes sense in their unique family circumstances, for all of the following reasons.

Respect and support are the foundation for a trusting relationship with our adult children and their partners.

While we may be perplexed with some of the methods that are being used to raise our grandchildren, we have to remember that the parents are in charge, and we are not the parents. We also need to acknowledge that there are new findings in child development and that parenting rules have changed (see Principle Three: Be Open to New Possibilities for some examples). Time and again, the young parents we interviewed stressed the importance of feeling that their parents had confidence in them and respected them in their role as parents.

For grandparents with a strained relationship with either their adult children or their children's partners, deciding to be an involved grandparent presents an opportunity to demonstrate maturity. In the experience of the grandparents we interviewed, the need to maintain a positive relationship with our grandchildren is usually more important than our need to be right. Many a grandboomer talked about the challenge of "saying nothing" when they were confronted with parenting approaches that, in their opinion, flew in the face of common sense, or were not in the best interests of the grandchildren or the family. In the words of one grandboomer, "I have learned to focus less on the issues and more on the pure joy of grandparenting."

For some families, the advent of grandchildren and the involvement and support from the grandparents have actually improved adult relationships. Peggy R. and Trina both talked about how the grandchildren had enriched their mother-daughter bond. While always close, these two intelligent and independent women had sometimes found themselves on opposite sides of an issue. Now, they are totally in sync when it comes to admiring and loving Trina's two daughters. They are also in concert in their appreciation and respect for each other in their respective roles as mother and "Nanny" to Maggie and Eve.

Of course, there is nothing like walking in another's shoes to understand their challenges. Like many grandparents, we have experienced feedback (the good, the bad, and the ugly) and appreciation from our adult children now that most of them are parents. And we love to admit they are better parents than we were in many ways. We hope that growing up with us has contributed in some small measure to their success!

A trusting relationship with the parents is the bridge to an open and rewarding relationship with our grandchildren.
Access to our grandchildren is generally through the parents. We can attempt to connect with our grandchildren by going around the parental bridge but this is a circuitous and dangerous path, fraught with dead ends, thorns, and swamps. A few of the young parents we interviewed were either disappointed or angered by the relationship with their parents or in-laws. Often this was because the grandparents were uninvolved, intrusive, or judgmental. Such was the case with Sean's parents.

> My parents are quite formal and from the "children should be seen and not heard" genre. They love our four children but whenever we visit they are constantly correcting their manners or trying to discipline them. Mom makes cryptic remarks about how it would be

so much better for the kids if Valerie stayed at home even though she knows that Valerie is very serious about her career. She doesn't understand that I am intentionally a very involved father. She thinks I am taking on Valerie's responsibilities whenever I parent. It has reached the point where neither Valerie nor I enjoy the visits and find ourselves making excuses to avoid them.

The relationship with the parents is especially important for grandparents on the father's side. Studies such as the National Longitudinal Survey of Children and Youth (NLSCY) confirm that there are two main determinants of closeness between children and their grandparents: proximity and family ties. Those grandparents who live closer, and the grandparents on the mother's side often have a closer relationship with their grandchildren. In our experience, the grandparenting bond on the father's side is greatly influenced by the effort invested in being there for both the parents and the grandchildren. We talked to many new parents who were very close to the grandparents on the father's side for this very reason. Claude talks about his parents.

Every summer Adrien and Alexandre spend four or five days with my mother and her husband. It is their special time and the memories are unforgettable: catching frogs, toasting marshmallows on the beach. They come back and talk about what happened two summers ago. My step-dad brings himself down to the kids' level. He rolls on the floor and always has a trick up his sleeve, either to distract them when they have a tantrum or to make them laugh. My mom is the one who cuddles and reads to them. The kids have formed memories that they will keep forever, like the ones I have with my grandfather.

Since less than 50 per cent of families remain intact, one of the main challenges many grandparents will face is maintaining relationships after divorce and separation (see Principle Four for more information). While we can't control the potential animosity and behaviours of our adult children and their former partners, we can control our own reactions. Another growth opportunity for grandparents! We need to be seen by our grandchildren as non-judgmental of either parent. Any grandparents hoping to continue their level of involvement with the grandchildren after the parents split up are wise to work hard at these relationships, particularly if the "ex" is the mother.

For Maria, her son's separation from his wife shortly after the birth of her granddaughter presented a real challenge.

> The split was not amicable but I was determined to maintain a relationship with my only granddaughter. I offered to babysit regularly and over the next seven or eight years I established a close bond with my granddaughter and her mother. This relationship became increasingly difficult when my son remarried and showed little interest in his daughter, while continuing to be hostile to her mother. I decided that my granddaughter's interests had to be uppermost. I continued to support her mother and made many efforts to involve my granddaughter in all family events. On occasion my son has not been happy with my choices but I feel that I made the right decision. I am very close to my granddaughter and have maintained a very good relationship with her mother. I walk a fine line between being a good grandmother and being a good mother.

Many new parents feel vulnerable and lack confidence in their role.
Our interviews confirmed the findings of the National Longitudinal Survey of Children and Youth (NLSCY), which shows that many new parents are struggling. Although the literature suggests that low-income and single parents are more likely to feel unprepared for the role, many two-income, two-parent families also feel overwhelmed by the new responsibilities and the pressure to be perfect parents. There is an explosion of parenting information available but some of it is conflicting or confusing. The fathers we talked with were not exempt

from the stress of trying to sort it all out, and sometimes felt unsure about their new role. Kevin, a successful entrepreneur and involved father with two young daughters, discussed his feelings openly.

> I love being a father but I sometimes feel a bit overwhelmed by the pressure. I give 100 per cent at my work and then I walk in the door and want to give 100 per cent as a father. The father's role is considered crucial but is not clearly defined. We are expected to be hands-on, involved, and proactive but must also be careful to protect and cherish the mother's role. It's a shifting road map for dads.

Not only are modern parents sometimes confused, they are also older and often tired. In the majority of families, both are employed outside the home (almost 70 per cent of women with children between zero and age eleven in the labour market). Today's parents report feeling time-crunched, trying to balance work and home life in a society that says it values the family, but does not yet provide adequate support for the parents of young children. It doesn't help when Grandma wonders aloud why Theo still has a bottle and isn't yet toilet trained at age three.

Grandparents can play a key role in relieving some of the stress young parents face. We can help in very practical ways, such as babysitting for an evening so that the parents can reconnect. We can also help by acknowledging our children's parenting skills. One young father summed it up so well:

> It is the little remarks and praise such as "you have really good instincts for mothering" or "you're such a natural father, so easy with the baby" that make a difference and give us confidence. Never underestimate your role as grandparents and the opportunity you have to be supportive and to build loving relationships, not only with your grandchildren but with your children as well.

In an atmosphere of trust and respect, parents are more likely to turn to the grandparents for the occasional bit of advice, or just for the opportunity to "sound out" their theories and challenges around child rearing. This is when we are wise to listen, be empathetic, and know when to share our point of view.

OVERCOMING THE BARRIERS

When we conducted our interviews and focus groups for this book, we consistently heard grandparents say that they found it difficult to hold back and bite their tongues. This held true across the spectrum of family situations. Whether our children and their partners are well-educated parents with whom we have an excellent relationship, or they are young, challenged, or estranged, we all have occasions when it is difficult to refrain from interjecting with a comment or suggestion about raising our grandchildren. There are a number of reasons we grapple with this principle. Perhaps by examining them, we can understand why it is sometimes so difficult to be the cheerleader instead of the quarterback.

Our egos

Sometimes, our egos get in the way. Not only did we raise children who became wonderful, competent young adults, but we also consider ourselves quite well informed about child development. We keep current, we are interested, and some of us actually have careers that overlap with the parenting field. Rosemary, a grandmother of four, suggests that grandparents need to put their egos aside and look at each situation from a fresh and unbiased point of view. If you still believe it is important to communicate a concern, time these conversations carefully. For example, while Rosemary feels that her daughter and her partner are sometimes too severe when disciplining their children, she refrains from commenting at the time of an incident and finds an appropriate opportunity to bring up her concern in a diplomatic way. Once she has expressed her opinion, she lets it go. The rest is up to the parents.

Our values

According to the American Association of Retired Persons (AARP) survey, the majority of grandparents consider one of their major roles is to pass on their values to their grandchildren. In our discussions with grandboomers, however, this was not a primary concern. In fact, most felt that shaping children's values was the responsibility of the parents, not the grandparents. Nonetheless, many boomers have deeply held values including religious and cultural beliefs that may not be as important for their children. How do we handle this?

Tracy's parents, whose lives centre on their family and church, decided not to interfere when Tracy and her husband did not baptize their first child. Their approach paid off in the long run.

> I am Catholic. My mom's sister is a nun and just celebrated her sixty-year jubilee. It took a long time to get the kids baptized and my parents handled it well. Family is first for them. When we are visiting them at their home, if the choice is going to church or staying with us, they always stay with us. The children were actually baptized in their church and they helped make it happen in a way that worked for us. The ceremony was very private. The church bent the rules. My parents kept their feelings about the children not being baptized from us until it was over. I felt supported, not pressured.

This example does not mean to imply that our children will always come around to our way of thinking, if we just remain patient. On the contrary, it is our experience that if we hold back, listen, and observe, we are just as likely to come around to theirs, or at least come to accept our differences (see Principle Four and Principle Ten for further discussion of this topic).

Our concerns for our grandchildren

Even when we are open and enlightened, some of the newer theories and practices may concern us, especially with the first grandchild: home births, infants sleeping on their backs, no solid foods until six months, and bed-sharing. Most of these practices are backed by solid evidence and we soon become acclimatized. Principle Three: Be Open to New Possibilities further explores how we as grandparents can learn more about new parenting practices.

Our concerns for our adult children

For a variety of reasons, some of us are still parenting our adult children. They are very young or parenting on their own. They have financial or emotional difficulties. We feel that they are too vulnerable to adequately take on full-time parenting at this time. When this is the case, grandparents may find themselves playing the dual role of parent and grandparent. The challenge is not to blur these lines. With the responsibility for providing extraordinary practical or financial support comes the feeling of entitlement to also make decisions and provide direction. This is natural, but not always helpful in the long run for our adult children. Grandparents need to be more of a coach than a director. Our adult children need to feel responsible and in control to develop as parents. The support has to come without a lot of strings attached.

Elizabeth describes how she met this challenge when her nineteen-year-old daughter and her boyfriend had a child while both were still in school.

These are young parents, still maturing. They are also from very different cultures. They need a lot of support until they finish their education. We pay the rent on their apartment and drive Kari to her daycare everyday, even though we are both still working. I often bite my tongue and try to let them make their own mistakes and grow in the process. It takes a village to support these kids. I provide my opinions when asked specific questions, but otherwise, I try not to interfere. I often feel stuck in the middle, trying to harmonize the two cultures. My strategy is to play the role of facilitator, not arbitrator. I pick my battles.

There are also grandparents who slip into the parenting role with their adult children out of habit not necessity, albeit with the best of intentions. We need to reflect on the impact of these interactions with our adult children, regardless of the intent. Do our actions demonstrate respect for them in their role as parents? How would we feel in their position? Are our habits as parents so deeply ingrained that we are unable to move to the next stage in our relationship with our children? According to Roberta Maisel, a sociologist, family mediator, and author, growing into a mature relationship with our adult children means letting go of long-standing behaviours and attitudes including:

- the need to be in control;
- the need to be right;
- the belief that we know more than our adult children;
- the idea that we know our children better than anyone else does;
- the need to help;
- the feeling of responsibility for our children's success or happiness.

The parents we interviewed were clear. Respect and support were paramount when they were asked what *they* needed most from their parents. How this plays out will be different for every family. The common thread is our willingness to be thoughtful and reflective, and to try and balance the needs of our adult children with our ability to respond, in a manner that honours us both. This is intentional grandparenting.

SOME SUGGESTIONS FROM PARENTS

During our interviews and focus groups, we asked young parents to tell us how grandparents could support them in their role. There were a number of recurring themes.

Encourage us

Emotional support was at the top of the wish list. Parents said:

- Tell us when we are doing a good job; praise me, praise my partner.
- Don't tell me how you handled things better.
- Be empathetic: try and understand how we feel.
- Be gentle: our lives are turned upside down, especially with the first baby; we have lots of doubts and questions.
- Be patient with us and our children. Being patient with my children is reassuring to us all. It's just so good to be with people who are crazy about our kids.

Communicate with us

Communication was seen as the key to mutual understanding between the parents and the grandparents. Parents said:

- Listen and understand where we are coming from.
- Ask us before assuming things, such as what are appropriate gifts.
- When you babysit, talk with us about "weekly or monthly issues." Is there something you as grandparents should watch out for or pay attention to; for example, what to do if our child goes through a food-throwing phase. (We take the food away.)
- Don't be a martyr: speak up! Tell us your expectations and if we are asking too much of you. Let us know what kind of grandparent you want to be.

Respect our parenting practices
Parents want grandparents to observe their parenting practices and follow their lead. Parents said:

- Spend time watching the family in action so you can see and understand how we handle issues.
- When you are with our children be consistent with things that are important to us, for example the use of "time outs" to discipline.
- If you don't understand something, ask; for example, how to buckle up the car seat properly. This is a major safety concern for us. Please take it seriously.
- Don't bribe grandchildren with cookies and candies instead of reasoning. Parents are then stuck with a child who expects a treat to conform to a behaviour.
- If you are giving advice, do so gently. Provide "gentle wisdom" without crossing the line of challenging how we want to parent.

Offer to babysit
Parents really appreciate this type of support. They said:

- We don't trust anyone else, especially for the first six months.
- We don't worry because we feel our parents can handle a crying baby.
- We need to be alone together as husband and wife. We simply don't get this time together if our parents are not available to babysit.
- There is a big role for grandparents when the second child comes along. Be prepared to help with the older child. He needs someone who knows and loves him. It is a big shock when Mom and Dad come home with a new sister or brother.

Be prepared

Parents were also very appreciative of grandparents who were well-prepared. They said:

- Childproof your house so we can relax there (no danger or fear the kids will hurt themselves or break precious knick-knacks).
- If possible, have a room and crib available when we visit, especially when coming from out of town. The baby sleeps better and so does the rest of the family. We worry about waking you up.

WHEN SPECIAL SUPPORT IS NEEDED

When a pregnancy is announced, all of us hope for a happy and healthy outcome. But this is not always the case. Many pregnancies end in miscarriage (one in five first-time pregnancies) and sometimes children are born with special needs. Postpartum depression (PPD) affects 10 per cent of new mothers. In all of these cases, grandparents can make a difference by offering both emotional and practical support.

In our experience, miscarriage is often handled as a private matter between the parents, especially if it occurs within the first twelve weeks. Because the probability of miscarriage is so high for women over thirty-five, many of the parents we talked to do not announce their pregnancy until they consider themselves past the risk period. Regardless of the timing, miscarriage is devastating for most parents, particularly so for older couples and those who have experienced more than one miscarriage. Grandparents can help ease the pain by being supportive and empathetic and by finding practical ways to help out, especially if there are other children in the family.

For Heather and Steve, parents of Alex, aged three, grandparents have a very valuable role to play when things don't go right.

> We've just recently lost our third baby, and I can tell you that I wouldn't be discussing this today if it wasn't for the support of my parents. I would be locked up in a padded room somewhere. My

parents have done everything from dealing with our grief to taking care of Alex on several occasions so that Steve and I had some time together to get our heads straight. They've hugged us, they've cooked for us, and they've taken care of the garden. They have been absolutely wonderful and they have listened to every one of my rants with patience and understanding.

I only recently realized how difficult all this has been for my parents as well. I told my mom that Steve and I were going to see a [baby-loss] counsellor to help us out, and she asked if they had a program for grandparents as well. I have been so wrapped up in my own loss that it never occurred to me how hard all this has been on them as well. They have been dealing with the grief of losing their grandchildren plus the heartbreak that comes with seeing your own child in despair. In my mind, grandparents are even more important in the bad times.

Grandparents can also play a supportive role when the family has special needs as a result of multiple births or children born with health problems. We talked to a number of families where the support of the grandparent in these situations made all the difference. When Brenda had twins after three months bedrest, her parents immediately stepped in to help. Her retired mother came over every day for the first three months, and half days for the next three. Her dad became the errand master. Not only did her mother provide full-time support, she also made considerable effort to understand the new ways of parenting so she could follow Brenda's lead.

There are many grandparents who are not in a position to drop everything and come to the support of their adult children. They may still be raising other children in the home, still working full-time, or, perhaps looking after their aging parents, as part of the sandwich generation. Or, they may live in another city. Despite these restrictions, many parents find a way to be supportive when their children are faced with special challenges. Joan, a consultant in international development, found herself in this position five years ago when her son and his wife had triplets.

> When the triplets were born early at thirty-two weeks, I was up to my neck in work. The babies remained in hospital for five weeks. When they came home from the hospital, my husband, Doug, went to Toronto for a week to help out. He pitched right in, feeding the babies and helping where he could. I was working to a deadline and went the following week. We continued to travel to Toronto every six weeks or so for the first year, staying a minimum of five days. At the same time, we had to cope with my aging mother. She felt neglected when we began to spend more time with the triplets than with her. It was a difficult juggling act, but the grandchildren were our priority. Doug finally had to talk to my mother about being more understanding.

Having a baby is a challenging time for women, both physically and emotionally. Many new mothers experience mood swings following delivery, feeling joyful one minute and tearful or sad the next. These "baby blues" usually pass within ten days with a little extra support and a few good nights' sleep. Some women may experience a deep and ongoing depression which lasts much longer and is known as postpartum depression (PPD). Because this syndrome is still poorly defined and under-researched, PPD often goes undiagnosed. Women are often reluctant to share how they are truly feeling because it doesn't fit their image of how things should be. Grandparents need to be aware of the symptoms of PPD so that they can offer support and reassurance. Postpartum depression can be treated effectively. Common approaches include therapy, support networks, and medications such as antidepressants.

Being a supportive grandparent isn't always easy or convenient. Our adult children and grandchildren often need us when we are busy, stressed, and under considerable work or family pressure ourselves. This is when we need to take a deep breath, confirm our priorities, and make decisions that support what is of prime importance in the long run. For most of us, that means family. We find a way to be there for our children and our grandchildren, especially in times of extraordinary need.

QUESTIONS AND ANSWERS

Q: Our daughter and her husband have a very traditional relationship: he works long hours to provide a comfortable lifestyle for them, and she looks after the house and family. This is fine until they visit us and it drives my wife and me crazy. He sits around reading, takes naps in the afternoon, seldom plays with his children, and lets us all wait on him hand and foot. What concerns us most is that we feel he is reneging on his role as a father. What can we do without alienating the parents?

A: It is not uncommon to find that sometimes our sons- and daughters-in-law don't quite live up to our standards as parents. We have to remember that we didn't raise them and are not responsible for their actions or value systems. And we aren't married to them.

It could be that your son-in-law sees visits with the grandparents as the only opportunity he has to take some time for himself. Try to develop a trusting relationship with your son-in-law and find opportunities to model and reinforce some of the behaviours that you value as a parent and grandparent. You are more likely to establish an open rapport with him in the long run if you focus on his strengths and build on these. It is like putting money in the relationship account. Once we have built up enough credit, the account won't be bankrupted by the occasional withdrawal, planned or otherwise.

Q: My wife and I are distressed with the amount of time our son and daughter-in-law allow our grandchildren to spend watching television and playing with their electronic games. Is there anything we can do about this without looking like we are criticizing the parents?

A: There is nothing you can do about the amount of time your grand-children are allowed to spend watching television and playing electronic games in their own homes. You can, however, have an influence on this when they visit you. Some grandparents find that it helps to talk with their grandchildren before they come over and to get agreement on which specific shows they will watch. The television stays off the rest of the time. Others have found that the best solution is to present your grandchildren with interesting alternatives. It's hard to watch TV when your grandpa takes you swimming or bowling!

WHAT THE RESEARCH TELLS US

Parents Are Key to Development
The National Longitudinal Survey of Children and Youth (NLSCY) has confirmed that effective parenting is one of the main determinants of overall health and well-being for children and youth, at all socio-economic levels. The first three years are especially critical. In particular, parental interaction with their children, and play-based problem-solving with other children during these first few years stimulate early brain development. No one can replace parents during this defining period, but we grandparents can play a significant role through our encourage-ment, support, and active participation.
Source: NLSCY. Human Resources Development Canada and Statistics Canada, 2002. www.statcan.ca/english/sdds/4450.htm

Loving Relationships Are Intergenerational
Tradition suggests that children are more likely to be emotionally close to grandparents on their mother's side. But a recent U.S. study showed that a grandchild's relationship with their grandparents on the father's side could be equally as close or closer. When adult children (whether they are men or women) are close to their own parents, their children are likely to be as well. Not surprisingly, caregiving by grandparents during

childhood was the other key factor in the quality of the relationship.
Source: Hess Brown, L. "Intergenerational Influences on Perceptions of Current Relationships with Grandparents," *Journal of Intergenerational Relationships*, 1 (1) (2003).

THE LAST WORD

We'd like to share the following words of wisdom around the childbirth process developed by a new father for his three male friends (Matt, Matt, and Pat) who were all "expecting" their first child within a month of each other. The list was developed a week after the birth of his daughter, Sienna.

Top Ten Things for Dads to Know about Childbirth
By Geoff Allan

10. Eat. Before going to the hospital, eat a lot and bulk up your reserves. You may be awake for the next twenty-four hours straight. Your time away from your wife will only be for brief periods, sometimes not long enough to eat much. You have to share the pain!
9. Pack well. You probably already know to bring your own food, snacks, etc., to the hospital. Your wife will ask you to get her stuff throughout labour. Don't forget a toothbrush.
8. Bring a book. You may start to feel useless and guilty watching your wife in pain. If you talk too much, it may get on her nerves. Your wife will simply want to know you are there. Get immersed in a good book to keep you occupied. Then, the minute she needs something, you are there.
7. Bring music. If you do not have a music system planned for the hospital room, I recommend you set one up, such as a portable CD player and PC speakers, at a minimum. Music enriches the mood and the right tunes add depth to your emotions.

6. Maintain a sense of humour. A bit of nervous energy sets in when you arrive at the hospital and get "set up." Relax, enjoy the ride, and keep your wife amused. It takes the edge off.

5. Massage. Yes, you will be massaging quite a lot, as you likely have already been doing. Be prepared for many hours of straight massaging.

4. Get on-line during recovery time. Some hospitals have direct-dial telephones or worst-case scenario operator intercepts, which still enable you to dial out using a PC. You may find it useful to bring a notebook computer, so that your wife can send e-mails during the recovery phase.

3. Capture it on film. Evaluate carefully if you want to videotape events pre-delivery. I recommend digital still photography only. When your wife is in recovery, make a video of the general situation and later edit in your still photography from the pre-delivery and delivery moments.

2. Vividly review your baby systems at home and establish the process flow of high-frequency activities, including diaper changes (have two complete stations), where you will sit when you hold the baby, washing the baby, etc.

1. Keep it personal. Upon arriving home, I recommend keeping your home private to you and your wife for at least twenty-four hours. Something happens when you get home alone with your wife and new child. The silence and the awe of the experience need to be absorbed. It's not New Year's Eve and you will be tired. But coming home together may be the most emotional period of the entire *accouchement*.

Be Open to
New Possibilities

There's an alternative. There's always a third way, and it's not a
combination of the other two ways. It's a different way.

— David Carradine

D o you remember when your children were teenagers? Peggy had
two signs posted on her refrigerator. One read: "Leave home now
while you still know everything!" The other said: "Mothers of teens
know why some animals eat their young."

Most parents breathe a sigh of relief when their rebellious adolescents
turn into responsible adults. The generation gap has finally disappeared
and we can now communicate as equals. That is until the magical
moment when your son or daughter calls to tell you they are expecting a
baby. Suddenly, the generation gap is back. Dr. Spock, Jolly Jumpers, and
old-style birthing are out. Baby whispering, seven-hundred-dollar three-
wheeled strollers, and natural childbirth with six attendants are in.

While the grandparents we talked with ranked Principle Three: Be
Open to New Possibilities lower on the list than some of the others,
they also admitted that accepting new ways of doing things could
sometimes be a cause of frustration and distress. Young parents on the
other hand were quite adamant that grandparents respect the new ways

of child rearing they believe in and practise. Sarah, a physician and young mother of three, summed it up this way:

> The big issues are always about sleep, food, and tantrums. We must realize that each generation has different philosophies about these things. For example, many grandparents are concerned that we put our babies to sleep on their backs. Yet there is solid evidence that this is the safest and best way for babies to sleep. My parents accept this and it amazes them that my children sleep even better than we did. My mom understands that things are different and has been supportive of the changes – but she still tries to give me advice on feeding my children.

Clearly, being open to new ways of doing things is essential to building positive relationships within the family. It is also good for grandparents themselves. Aging boomers who stop learning or cease to be curious about new developments get stagnant and cranky. Their children have every right to feel that they are stuck in the past.

At the same time, grandparents know from experience that while some changes are good, others are just fads. As discussed in the previous chapter, we might worry that some new ways of doing things make parenting more difficult or could even be harmful to either the child or the parents. It is painful to watch our grown-up babies struggle with their babies, and to stay quiet when we know there is an easier way.

Most experts suggest that there is a middle ground. As a grandparent, you have wisdom and experience that can be helpful and comforting. The trick is in how and when you provide suggestions and advice. Grandparents who are supportive and respectful will likely find that their adult children will ask them for advice, or at least will want to "try out" child-rearing ideas and concerns that are troubling them.

This chapter focuses on changes related to pregnancy, birth, and early child rearing. This does not mean that this principle ceases to apply as your grandchildren get older. In fact, being open to new ways of doing things remains equally important as our grandchildren go through school and grow into adolescence. Examples of how grandparents can be open to new ideas about child rearing with older children can be found throughout other chapters. Principle Four also deals with being open to new possibilities by exploring the dramatic changes in family types, living arrangements, and culture.

Maternity traditions, birthing, and child rearing have changed a lot in the last forty years, as the chart below demonstrates.

THEN AND NOW
YOU'VE COME A LONG WAY, BABY!

1964	1974	2004
Popular Names		
Michael, Mary	Jason, Jennifer	Liam, Brianna
Maternity Wear		
Demure, loose dresses with Peter Pan collars	Flowered empire dresses with miniskirts; bell-bottom maternity pants	Stretchy, tight "show your belly off" tops, skirts, and pants; bikini bathing suits
Maternity Ward		
Drug-assisted delivery	Epidurals, "rooming in"	Natural childbirth or Caesarean
In hospital 14 days	In hospital 5–7 days	In hospital 24-48 hours

1964	1974	2004
No fathers allowed in delivery room	Fathers sometimes allowed in	Birthing rooms, Dad assists and cuts cord
Mom gets enema and is shaved from belly button to knees	Mom gets enema and pubic area is shaved	No shaving or enemas
Placenta whisked away	Mom buries placenta in her garden	Some parents cook and eat the placenta for its nutritional and symbolic value (true!)

Advice on Child Rearing

Baby and Child Care by Dr. Benjamin Spock	*Your Baby and Child: From Birth to Age Five* by Penelope Leach	*What to Expect When You're Expecting* by Heidi Murkoff, Arlene Eisenberg, and Sandee Hathaway
Feed on demand; follow child's lead	Stop, listen, and learn from your children	Part of a series; month-by-month details; focuses on worries and lists answers to hundreds of questions

---

1964	1974	2004
Advice on Feeding		
Bottled formula or breast-feed; introduce Pablum early	Breast- or bottle-feed 3–6 months; make your own baby food	Breast-feed 6 months (no solids); pump your milk for when you are not there
The Latest Wheels		
Large, traditional English prams (cost $150–$200)	Umbrella strollers ($14.95)	Three-wheeler deluxe running strollers ($500–$700)
Toys, Toys		
Wooden blocks and puzzles	Plastic stacking boxes, farms, and school buses	Tiny soft cloth blocks and animals
Barbie makes her debut	Barbie goes out to work	Barbie's best friend, Midge, gets pregnant and grand-parent dolls are created
Best-Selling Children's Book		
Green Eggs and Ham by Dr. Seuss	*Love You Forever* by Robert Munsch	*Walter the Farting Dog* by William Kotzwinkle and Glenn Murray

MODERN PARENTS, PREGNANCY, AND BIRTH

It's amazing how many grandboomers have ultrasound photographs of baby-to-be posted proudly on their refrigerators or as screen savers on their home computers. The use of ultrasound imaging throughout pregnancy is just one of the modern practices that are now commonplace. Parents, siblings, and grandparents can now watch the miracle of fetal development and keep it for posterity in their photo albums.

There are pros and cons to the use of **new technologies** associated with pregnancy and birth. Ultrasound images, for example, quite often reveal the sex of baby-to-be, which some people feel is advantageous, while others do not. The increased use of prenatal testing such as amniocentesis and associated genetic counselling raises ethical concerns for some, and sometimes unnecessary worries for expectant couples. Most professionals and parents believe that fetal monitoring, which requires the mother to be hooked up to a machine and mostly stay in bed throughout labour, is essential to knowing if the baby is in distress. Yet, the use of this unnatural inconvenience in uncomplicated labours is disputed among the experts.

Most young parents now make "birth plans" ahead of time. They include whether or not Mom will have an episiotomy, take medication, or wants a "natural" childbirth, and how Dad will assist – including vaginal massage.

Should a grandparent be concerned and read up about these technological issues related to birth? Absolutely. We all want the best outcome and experience for both the parents and the baby. Should you discuss the birthing plan with the prospective parents? Only if they wish to talk about it. Your role here is to support their decisions while stressing that birth plans may change when labour starts, and that they should not feel inadequate or guilty if it does not go exactly as planned. Should we try to influence their thinking? Probably not. While it is fine to express your wish for the best possible outcome, these kinds of decisions rest with the parents and their health-care providers.

Some of the greatest technological advances of the twenty-first century relate to assisted reproduction and the survival of high-risk infants. Specialized surgery and neonatal units can now save babies who arrive too early or who are born with complications that could not be treated thirty years ago. Fertility treatments and assisted reproduction such as in vitro fertilization are wonderful advances for couples that cannot become pregnant. They have also led to significant increases in the number of multiple births. Like other high-risk babies, these infants are often tiny and may need special care in hospital for a period of time.

Grandparents need to be ready to support parents when early-warning signs suggest there are concerns about the health of the infant or infants and when special care is required after the birth. Hospitals and physicians encourage new parents (and often grandparents) to come to the hospital and spend as much time with the new baby as possible. This is rewarding but emotionally and physically draining for all involved. The new mom is especially vulnerable as she tries to recover from the pregnancy and birth while dealing with fatigue, plummeting hormones, and worry, all at the same time. When baby is released from hospital, special care may be required at home. With twins or triplets, the workload and fatigue is doubled or tripled.

In cases like this, grandparents need to figure out how they can be most supportive while the baby is in hospital and when he comes home. For example, you may decide to spend time at the hospital, to free up the parents by looking after other children, or to offer to assist with errands, driving, cleaning, or shopping.

When their son and daughter-in-law had a high-risk newborn that needed special care at home, Paul and Valerie decided that one of the best ways they could help was to initiate their own "meals on wheels" program.

We delivered a hot, healthy dinner to our children's home five nights a week. We never lingered, just rang the bell and left it for them with a hug and a kiss. The next night we would bring another and pick up the dirty dishes. Later, our daughter-in-law told us that it was the best thing we could have done, that it made their lives so much easier not to even have to think about preparing and cooking a meal each night.

The **social and cultural changes** related to pregnancy and childbirth may be even greater than the technological changes that have occurred in the past thirty years. The most significant change has been in the father's role. Today's dad is expected to be very involved in the pregnancy, birth, and raising of his child. Fathers commonly attend prenatal checkups and classes with their wives. They prepare themselves by reading numerous books, including a few that are directed specifically to fathers. They act as coaches and helpers during the birth. Many sleep in the hospital room afterwards and help look after baby and Mom. Most take parental leave when baby comes home and they remain equal partners with Mom in raising the children. Some fathers reduce their work hours (with a subsequent reduction in pay or promotion opportunities) in order to spend more time at home with their children. Some even take on the role of primary caregiver while their wives head back to work full-time.

Everyone we spoke with supported these changes. Grandfather Phil expressed his pride and philosophical thinking behind the involved role that his son was playing as a new father.

Many of us regret that we missed out in the early years because we were too busy working. I am really proud to see my son so involved. It is good for him, for his wife, and for their children. I feel like it is a natural progression that has been occurring over time. I was more involved as a parent than my father. My son is more involved than I was. It's been a dramatic, positive evolution in the man's role in the family. And I welcome it.

Another area that has changed dramatically is the **location and atmosphere of the birth experience**. With increased support for midwifery in North America, the number of home births has increased. In rare cases, some deliveries even occur underwater (an increasingly popular practice in Europe). Most often, today's births no longer occur in delivery rooms but in hospital birthing rooms that are made to look and feel like living rooms or regular hospital rooms, with the birthing equipment hidden in a closet. Fathers and other birth supporters are given cots so they can sleep in the room. Mom is free to take a shower or bath at will and to eat food brought in from outside. After the birth, baby stays in the same room in a little bassinet on wheels.

In addition to the expanded role of the father, the number and types of people involved in childbirth have changed dramatically (see the chart below for a description of who's who and who does what on the childbirth team).

THE CHILDBIRTH TEAM

- *Prenatal educators* are most often nurses who provide parents-to-be with practical information about pregnancy and childbirth.
- *Obstetrician-gynecologists* have five years of specialized training on top of a medical degree. Most women are referred to these specialists by their family doctor after the first trimester. He or she will be affiliated with a specific hospital, where the mom-to-be will deliver her baby.
- *Registered midwives* have completed a four-year university degree plus additional training. They provide care from the early stages of pregnancy until six weeks after birth. They have hospital privileges and can be counted on to be there during delivery.
- *Doulas* are certified by Doulas of North America or The Childbirth and Postpartum Professional Association of Canada.

Doulas provide physical, emotional, and informational support before, during, or after childbirth.

- *Lactation consultants* are often but not always nurses. Some work at breast-feeding clinics in hospitals and public-health offices; others are in private practice. They provide advice and practical help with breast-feeding.
- *Case-room nurses* include those who specialize in labour-and-delivery, and in postpartum care.
- *Public health nurses* provide advice and help after new moms are home from the hospital, through telephone and home visits.

One grandfather described how he dealt with his concerns about the well-being of his stepdaughter, when she and her husband opted to have a doula present at the birth of their first child.

> I had never heard of a doula before. I was anxious about how things would go. It seemed to me that the delivery room would be crowded with people, but no mention had been made of a qualified physician being present. I was really concerned about Catherine's safety and well-being. Would there be anyone there who was legally and medically qualified to deal with an emergency? Eventually, I decided to do some research. I looked on the Internet and read up on the childbirth team, including doulas. I talked with Catherine and was reassured that she did indeed plan to have a doctor present. I relaxed and accepted this new development. In the end, all went smoothly and I felt totally comfortable with the care and support Catherine received. Being there was one of the most wonderful experiences of my life.

Early release from hospital (often within twenty-four to forty-eight hours) has increased the stress on new families when they arrive home with their new baby. Moms leave hospital before their milk is fully in and there is little chance for a nurse to help her become effective at breast-feeding. Gone are the days when new moms had time in hospital to learn and get comfortable with routines such as bathing and swaddling. Common problems such as jaundice used to be routinely taken care of in baby wards by shining lights on the baby to help relieve the problem. Now, many parents panic when baby looks slightly yellow when they get home, or when a baby boy's scrotum continues to be bright red and swollen. Unless they have had an opportunity to learn about these kinds of things in a prenatal class or through independent reading, or are lucky enough to have home visits from a public-health nurse or midwife, new parents may understandably feel frightened or overwhelmed. Often the first call they make is to Grandma.

BARRIERS TO BEING OPEN

We asked other grandboomers what makes it difficult to put this principle into practice, and how they overcome these barriers.

I believe that I was a competent parent. If things worked for me, why do they have to be different now?
Let's face it. All of us resist change to some extent, especially when our experience tells us otherwise. Jane talks about how she handles this feeling and the fact that our children have access to a lot of new information that we did not have.

> I decided that if I was going to be supportive and relevant, I had to read the same books that my daughter and her husband were reading. I surfed the Net for information about new trends and child-rearing practices. Then, I felt knowledgeable enough to discuss some of these issues with the parents.

Some health professionals are quite rigid about the new "rules" related to pregnancy, natural childbirth, and breast-feeding. I am worried about the well-being of my daughter (or daughter-in-law) because she believes she must live up to these guidelines.

Marion describes how she dealt with her concerns when her daughter insisted on breast-feeding only, despite the fact she was having trouble.

> Susan was in tears when she called. One of her nipples was badly infected and the baby would only suck on that side. My first reaction was to suggest she use a bottle, that breast-feeding did not work for everyone. After all, I bottle-fed all of my children, and they thrived. But Susan was adamant. All the experts had told her that she should feed her child only breast milk for six months. She wanted to do it "right." Then I remembered that a friend's daughter had received a lot of help from a lactation consultant. I told Susan how much I loved her and asked her to put her husband on the line. I suggested he phone the Public Health Department and ask about finding a lactation consultant.
>
> The next day my son-in-law called to say that they had been referred to La Leche League International and a lactation consultant had come right away. Susan had been sent to her doctor to treat the infection, and the consultant had showed her how to help the baby latch on to the other breast. The crisis was over.

Some of the new ideas and practices make me concerned about the health and safety of my grandkids. Fads can be harmful, especially when they ignore what seems to be common sense.
Nancy was concerned because her daughter and son-in-law took a lot of food supplements, and they were now giving these to her three-year-old granddaughter.

> At first I just kept my mouth shut. I knew that eating habits can be a real source of conflict in families. But I worried about what was in some of the stuff. I read that we shouldn't trust supplements that come from China and other places that don't have the regulations we have here. It didn't seem to be harming the parents, but Cindy was only three! Finally, I called Health Canada. They

directed me to their Web site for some guidelines on these kinds of products, and on feeding preschoolers (www.hc-sc.gc.ca and www.dietitians.ca/healthystart). They also said that there was a free dial-a-dietitian service available. I told my daughter about these resources and she looked them up. As a result, they made some changes in the supplements they were taking themselves, as well as some healthy changes in how they were feeding Cindy. I was relieved and happy that I had not provoked a confrontation.

THE "OLD" METHOD OF ASSESSING NEW PRACTICES

If you are wondering what to do about a new child-rearing practice that concerns you, try using the acronym OLD, which stands for "Observe," "Learn," and "Decide."

Observe: As stressed in Principle Two, let the parents take the lead. Observe how they go about things and support them in their decisions, whenever possible.

Learn: Once you are clear about the birthing or child-rearing practice in question, do your research. Read the latest books, surf reliable sources on the Net, and ask professionals who specialize in health and child development. You will find that most issues fall into one of three categories:

1) they are good practices that are based on solid evidence;
2) the evidence is unclear but they do no harm;
3) there is no evidence to support the practice and it may make things more difficult or even harmful for the child or the parents or both.

(See the section "What the Research Tells Us" at the end of this chapter for some examples.)

Decide: Once you are fully informed on the issue, determine how you will act. In most cases, other grandparents told us that they supported the parents' decisions because they were based on new and solid information, or they appeared to be harmless. If a certain practice or philosophy remains worrisome, you may want to talk about it with the parents. Present your concern in a non-judgmental and rational way, based on what you have learned. If the parents are open to your views, talk it through. Otherwise, leave it with them to decide what they will do with your information.

Note: While none of the families we interviewed had encountered a situation involving real harm, it goes without saying that grandparents, like all responsible citizens, must step in to protect a child and/or parent in cases of harmful abuse or neglect. Health professionals and school and daycare workers are required by law to report all suspected cases of child abuse to a local child protection agency.

NEW CHILD-REARING PRACTICES AND CHILD DEVELOPMENT

Most child-rearing advice today is solidly built on the research in healthy child development carried out in the last ten years. This includes exciting research on brain development and the natural attachments that occur between children and loving adults.

Thanks to brain-imaging techniques, we now know that the higher centres of the brain – those that control the emotions, language, thinking, and the capacity for problem solving – develop gradually from birth until the end of adolescence. During this time, the brain actively makes connections, called synapses, between individual nerve cells, and combines these connections into pathways. Most of these pathways are established during the first few years of life. In fact, some important "windows of opportunity" governing intellectual and emotional functioning are programmed to close by the end of the first three years. So while changes can still occur (because people continue to be influenced by their environments throughout their lives), early childhood experiences have a particularly important effect on subsequent behaviour and well-being.

What does this mean for child rearing and grandparenting? While some brain functions continue to develop into adolescence, optimal "hard-wiring" of the brain depends to a large extent on whether or not parents (and others such as grandparents) provide enough of the needed kinds of stimulation, and not too much of the wrong kinds, in the first three years of life. For example, the area of the brain governing vocabulary development (a prerequisite for learning to speak, read, write, learn, and reason effectively) will develop if the child receives enough emotional, cognitive, and language stimulation during the early years. If not, that area will remain underdeveloped. Parents (and others) can give infants and young children this essential stimulation by talking and singing to them, by playing word games and reading stories, and by actively teaching them words and ideas.

QUESTIONS AND ANSWERS

Q: We would love to be present at the birth of our grandchild. Is this appropriate? How should we bring this up with our children?

A: The historically common practice of grandmothers attending the birth of their grandchildren has been out of favour for many years. Happily, this is changing again. Many parents and hospitals now welcome the presence of both grandmothers and grandfathers during the birth or shortly after. This is totally appropriate, as long as the parents and birth assistants agree.

The key is to talk with the parents about their plans for the birth and immediately after. They may be open to your attendance at the birth or, what is more common, to having you wait outside the room until baby has arrived. Some parents may see the birth as a private experience to be shared by them alone, or they may not want to have to concern themselves with other family members at this intense time.

Sometimes, the medical team may feel it is too crowded already or they may have concerns about the possibility of complications calling for emergency procedures. It is important to talk about all of these concerns ahead of time.

If the parents want you in attendance, make every effort to get there, even if it means dropping everything to jump on a plane. Every grandparent we talked with who was fortunate enough to be in attendance at the birth or shortly after spoke of it as a "thrilling" and "magic" moment.

Sandy describes how she and her husband waited outside the room while their daughter was in the last stages of labour and birth.

> We were peeking through the door and saw the nurse cleaning and swaddling this little person. We could just see our tired but happy daughter, and her sister and husband who were grinning from ear to ear. The doctor opened the door and placed our new grandson in Grandpa's arms while she attended to our daughter. His eyes filled with tears and he began to gently rock the baby back and forth. Then it was my turn. Holding this tiny miracle and feeling the love we all shared felt like a sacred moment. Then I went to my stepdaughter. I kissed her and told her what a wonderful and beautiful mother she was, and what a fabulous job she had done. We hugged and cried a little. There is no doubt that this was one of the most profound experiences of my life. It is a memory that will stay with me forever.

Q: We are the parents of the expecting father. Should we defer to the parents of the mother when it comes to attending the birth?

A: Again, the key is to talk openly with the parents ahead of time and ask them what they want to happen. It is natural for the mother-to-be to favour her own mother's attendance at the birth or immediately after (it may be too crowded or tiring to have both sets of grandparents present).

On the other hand, they may invite you to be there, or to play an important role looking after other children while they are at the hospital.

Q: Should we visit the new parents when they come home with the baby to help out?

A: If you live in the same city, you can help in very practical and non-intrusive ways, such as running errands, bringing hot meals, helping look after other children in the family, or short visits that can include a brief chat or taking the baby out for a walk. It becomes a bigger question if you need to travel and move in with the new family. In both cases, however, the answer once again is: check with the parents as to how they want to handle the first few weeks they are home with baby. Since many fathers now take parental leave, most young parents today prefer to have time alone to adjust. Others, like Deborah who gave birth to twins, are more than happy to have a grandmother, grandfather, or both around to help out.

> My mother-in-law lives in Egypt and speaks almost no English. When she offered to come and help us after the birth of the twins, I was a bit concerned. It turned out to be the best possible solution. She spent the whole day singing, cooking, cleaning, washing baby clothes, and helping me nurse the twins. We communicated with smiles, hand gestures, and some limited knowledge of each other's languages. Her positive, happy nature filled the house with joy and the smells of her traditional cooking made both my husband and I ravenous for a well-prepared hot dinner every night.

WHAT THE RESEARCH TELLS US

In bold below are ten current beliefs and practices related to pregnancy and infants and what the experts say about them. Use the OLD method described in this chapter to help you come to your own conclusions about other new possibilities you encounter. When the evidence is unclear, encourage the parents to go with what feels right for them in their particular situation.

1. All women of child-bearing age should take folic acid supplements, especially if planning to become pregnant.
Yes, taking folic acid supplements prior to and during the early stages of pregnancy greatly reduces the risk of spina bifida, a congenital defect of the spine.

2. Women should refrain from smoking or drinking alcohol during pregnancy.
Yes, even occasional smoking and exposure to second-hand smoke can negatively affect the development of the fetus. Because we do not know precisely what level of alcohol use is safe, experts recommend none at all.

3. Always put baby on his back to sleep.
Yes, sleeping baby on the back significantly reduces the risk of sudden infant death syndrome (SIDS). (This is a complete reversal of what parents were told in the 1970s.)

4. It is safe and beneficial for parents and baby to sleep in the same bed.
Expert opinion varies. Some research shows that it enhances bonding and breast-feeding; other studies show an increased risk that baby may suffocate and that parents may become seriously sleep-deprived. Parents need to decide what works best for them in their situation.

5. Infant car seats (up to forty pounds) and then booster seats that meet stringent government-approved standards must be used, even when travelling short distances.
Yes, approved infant and booster seats significantly reduce the risk of serious injury or death in the event of a crash. Motor-vehicle accidents

are the number-one cause of death in young children. BE VIGILANT. Learn how to use child restraints properly and always buckle up.

6. Listening to classical music in utero and in infancy will boost a child's IQ (the Mozart effect).

Follow-up studies failed to replicate the original results and child-development experts remain skeptical that listening to Mozart will change IQ. However, exposing babies and young children to music (especially lullabies) is soothing and causes no harm. In addition, it is well accepted that singing and making up songs with very young children encourages creativity and imagination.

7. Never give a baby or young child a bottle of milk or juice to take to bed.

Yes, going to sleep with milk or juice in the mouth harms a young child's teeth and gums. This is called the "baby-bottle syndrome." Plain water and soothers do no harm.

8. Do not feed babies any solid foods until six months.

The American Academy of Pediatrics and other expert groups recommend that parents not introduce solids before six months of age. Introducing cereal or other starter foods too early can cause digestive problems such as gas and loose stools or constipation. However, many parents start solids earlier than six months with no ill effects. The experts suggest that parents talk with a pediatrician about what is best in individual cases.

9. Do not give infants honey and do not give children peanuts for the first three years.

No more honey on the soother, Grandma! Honey can harbour spores of *Clostridium botulinum* (botulism), which can grow and produce life-threatening toxins in a baby's intestinal tract.

Peanuts can cause violent allergic reactions. They're also a choking hazard. To be on the safe side, experts recommend no peanuts or peanut butter until a child is three years old, especially if either parent has a history of peanut allergies.

10. Adults should not spank a child.
Experts agree that spanking, hitting, and shaking are inappropriate ways to discipline a child, that may cause serious physical and/or emotional harm. Discipline should be used to help children learn appropriate behaviour, not to punish them. Removing a child from the stressful environment or using the "time out" technique are better ways to teach a child self-control. Parents and grandparents who find themselves losing control when a child misbehaves should call a friend or support service for help to calm down.

THE LAST WORD
Some grandparents cringe when they hear about the many restrictions placed on children today. One sent us the following remembrance of the "carefree days."

> Remember when we were growing up? According to today's regulators and bureaucrats, those of us who were kids in the 1940s, '50s, and '60s probably shouldn't have survived.
>
> Our baby cribs were hand-me-downs. We had no childproof lids on medicine bottles, doors, or cabinets, and when we rode our bikes, we had no helmets. (Not to mention the risks we took hitchhiking.) Our parents rarely buckled us up in the car and there were no air bags. Riding in the back of a pickup truck on a warm day was always a special treat.
>
> We drank water from the garden hose and shared one soft drink with four friends. We ate cupcakes, bread and butter, and drank soda pop with sugar in it, but we were (almost) never overweight because we were always outside playing. We would leave

home in the morning and play all day. No one was able to reach us – no cellphones.

We did not have Playstations, Xboxes, DVDs, video games, cellphones, iPods, Internet chat rooms, or TV with more than three channels. We walked to a friend's home and rang the bell, or just walked in and talked to them.

We fell out of trees and off the playground equipment, got cut, and broke bones and teeth, and there were no lawsuits from these accidents. We made up games with sticks and tennis balls. We didn't have Little League tryouts. Anyone who wanted to play, played. No adults stood around telling us how to do it; we figured out rules that suited us.

Despite it all, we survived, even prospered. And most of us treasure our memories of a carefree childhood.

It kind of makes you want to run through the house with scissors!

Embrace Diversity

The family. We were a strange little band of characters trudging through life sharing diseases and toothpaste, . . . inflicting pain and kissing to heal it in the same instant, loving, laughing, defending, and trying to figure out the common thread that bound us all together.

— Erma Bombeck

Over the last two generations there have been dramatic changes in marriage, family structures, and parenthood. These trends are causing people to alter their perception of marriage and families, and to broaden their definitions of these terms. At the same time, new waves of immigrants and refugees from Asia, Africa, and the Middle East have added to the cultural and ethnic diversity of North America. This has contributed to a dramatic growth of visible minorities, particularly in Canada, and to an increase in interfaith and interracial marriages.

Principle Three deals with the importance of being open to new opportunities related to childbirth and child rearing. In this chapter we explore the need for grandboomers to be open to new types of family structures and diverse cultures. Indeed, Principle Four suggests that in the twenty-first century we need to go beyond openness, to embrace diversity and celebrate the arrival of our grandchildren no matter what their family looks like.

THEN AND NOW
A number of important trends in our society are having a dramatic impact on what we know as family. Let's look at how families have changed since we were young.

Marriage and Divorce
Marriage has changed significantly in the last hundred years. A century ago, couples lived apart until marriage, which was a commitment for life. Only a very small percentage of people divorced. Now, about 50 per cent of all marriages end in divorce. Most committed couples in North America live together before marriage and many remain in common-law arrangements. In Quebec, for example, living together is now the norm rather than the exception. Some couples have decided to pursue two careers and to have no children. More women are having children outside of marriage and surrogate motherhood is increasing. Same-sex unions are more common and same-sex marriage is now legal in parts of Canada.

Single Parenting
In the U.S., the percentage of children who live with a single parent has tripled in the last forty years: from 9 per cent in 1960 to 27 per cent in 2000. In Canada, some 16 per cent of children live in single-parent households. In the great majority of cases, single parents are female. Some are young, never-married moms; some are single career-women who have chosen to parent alone. Others are mothers who have been separated or divorced. In this case, single parenting may be fairly short-term, since most divorced people tend to remarry or enter into another live-in relationship.

Irene and Don talk about their unique situation as grandparents. Their daughter's first child was born when she was a young single parent still living at home. Now, some twelve years later, they have a second grandchild born to the same daughter and her husband of over ten years.

> We helped raise our grandson Craig on a day-to-day basis. We were more like backup parents than grandparents. When my daughter moved in with her current partner, it was hard to let go of the parenting role. We still want to be involved in everything Craig does, and sometimes forget that it is not our job to discipline him in his parents' home. Things are totally different with the new baby. We are clear about our role for that one.

Blended Families

Most parents find a new long-term relationship after divorce or the dissolution of a common-law union. This results in the phenomenon of blended families, when children from different parents share a home full- or part-time with a stepfather or stepmother. It also leads to large extended families, including as many as eight sets of grandparents and sometimes multiple great-grandparents. You may inherit a new grandchild that you meet for the first time at age twelve. Extended families can lead to logistical nightmares at events such as baptisms, bar mitzvahs, graduations, and weddings. But in the end, parents who love their adult children and want to have a role in the lives of all their grandchildren will find a way to do so.

Peggy recalls how she felt when she went to visit her daughter Patty at the hospital after the birth of her second child, Andrew.

> The nurse told me that Patty was in the sunroom with the baby and some visitors. I arrived there to find three great-grandmothers cooing over Andrew. It made no difference to my mother, my ex-mother-in-law, and my current mother-in-law that Patty's dad and I were no longer together. They were all there to celebrate the birth of their granddaughter's child. I felt the love, excitement, and

acceptance in the room. I knew then that blended families can be good for children because there are more people to love and care for them!

Adoption

After decades of secrecy, adoption has come out of the closet. In addition to couples with fertility problems and those in same-sex relationships, more and more parents with biological children are turning to adoption as a way to expand their families. The number of adoptions by single people is increasing and foster-care reform has greatly improved the chances of older children finding permanent, adoptive homes.

Ironically, at the same time that the number of people wanting to adopt has increased, fewer babies are available. Access to contraception and abortion, as well as society's acceptance of what used to be called "unwed" mothers have reduced the number of American and Canadian infants available for adoption. As a result, more families are turning to international adoptions, which may cost as much as twenty-five thousand dollars.

Sandra and Dan describe how they provided emotional and practical support to their son and his wife, who decided on an international adoption after finding out that they were infertile.

We suggested that they apply to the Hebrew Free Loan Association for an interest-free adoption loan and that they deal with a reputable agency. All of us were worried that the child might have developmental problems because of neglect in early life. When they received a video and medical report from Russia about two-year-old Katja, they took them to a pediatrician for his review and advice. While Katja was underweight and slightly behind in her development, the doctor said she was essentially very healthy. We reassured them in the weeks of waiting that followed. We drove them to the airport and picked them up when they came home with Katja. Today, she is a happy, well-adjusted seven-year-old. We were right to trust our instincts and the decisions that our children made. I know parents whose biological children have problems. Let's face it – there are no guarantees with any child.

Same-Sex Unions and Parenting

Until recently, same-sex couples could not marry anywhere in the world. This changed in 2001 when Holland enlarged its definition of marriage to include same-sex couples. Two years later, Belgium and several provinces in Canada followed suit. In 2004, in the United States, only a man and a woman can have their marriage recognized by the state.

Whether or not the courts and politicians in various jurisdictions decide to sanction same-sex marriages, same-sex unions are becoming more common and open in society. Same-sex couples are demonstrating their commitment to a long-term loving relationship in the same way that heterosexual couples do. Many of them wish to become parents and are doing so, either through adoption or in vitro fertilization with an anonymous donor.

When our children enter into a same-sex relationship, their children become our grandchildren. They need and deserve the same support and unconditional love that we give to grandchildren born in a more traditional marriage or common-law relationship.

Jeanne and Maurice talk about how thrilled they are to have grandchildren from their daughter's lesbian relationship.

We have known for a long time that our only child, Louise, is a lesbian. When she decided to share her life with Shirley, we inherited two wonderful grandchildren from Shirley's previous marriage. Louise and Shirley built a home down the street from us. The children come to our place for lunch every day. Their parents are involved and welcome at the school and in the community. We had always dreamed of having grandchildren but had thought it was not a possibility. What an unexpected and happy surprise for all of us.

Biracial and Immigrant Families

It is hard to believe that it was only in 1967 that mixed-race couples were allowed to marry anywhere in the U.S. Today, the number of biracial and intercultural unions in both the United States and Canada is significant and continues to increase. This trend, combined with the increase in foreign adoptions, means that many of us will grandparent children that have different skin colours and physical features than our own.

Pauline has four Caucasian children. Two of them have black partners. She talks about how her biracial grandchildren are no different than the others.

A grandchild doesn't have to have the same skin colour or facial features to be yours. I was raised to believe that everyone is the same. The love I feel is the same with all of my grandkids. In fact, I forget that some of them have darker skin than the others. Each of my fourteen grandchildren is unique and special – because of their different likes, moods, and personalities. It has nothing to do with how they look.

Many grandchildren from immigrant families have few opportunities to visit grandparents who live in the home country. Sometimes, a Canadian or American family comes forward to help out, as described by Karla, now aged twenty-three.

Mrs. Connie and Doug kind of "adopted" my mom when she escaped to Canada when the Russian tanks rolled into Prague. They helped her adjust to a new life and stayed in touch after she married. When my brother and I were born, they "adopted" us too, as their grandchildren. I'm very lucky. I could look forward to occasionally visiting my real grandmother in the Czech Republic and I had my Canadian grandparents to love and support me here.

CHALLENGES RELATED TO FAMILY DIVERSITY

While all of us like to think of ourselves as open to diverse families and cultures, the grandparents we spoke with identified some of the challenges with putting this principle into practice.

Conflicting beliefs

Some grandboomers inevitably encounter a conflict in beliefs and values in the event of inter-religious and intercultural marriages. Some have difficulty with same-sex unions and young adults' choices to parent alone, divorce, or live common-law. Grandparents who talked about these issues suggested that "acceptance" and "tolerance" were key in these situations.

Michael, whose Catholic daughter married a young man raised in the Jewish faith, explains what tolerance means to him.

> Being tolerant does not require me to accept another religion as true. It does mean that I have to respect my son-in-law's right to his own beliefs, and the parents' right to bring up their children as they see fit. His side of the family is tolerant too. It all started at the wedding when the young couple combined his traditions and ours in an interfaith service. Now they celebrate both Christmas and Hanukkah with the children. My grandchildren have taught me a lot about the Jewish faith that I didn't know before, and my initial reservations are pretty well gone. You know, tolerance is really only the first step toward embracing different points of view, but it is a step that many families have yet to take.

In the words of Jeanne, whose daughter and lesbian partner are raising two children, "We have a higher moral obligation – to put our own conflicted feelings aside for the good of our precious grand-children."

"Instant" step-grandparenting due to remarriage

Since most couples who divorce or separate tend to remarry, many grandparents will find themselves "instant" step-grandparents. There is no time to prepare. Sometimes the children are older. You do not know their family of origin or how they have been brought up. The birth family may see you as an interloper, especially if one of the parents was abandoned in favour of your son or daughter. There is now a potential of numerous grandparents for each child. The children may be going through a lot of emotional issues related to the new family situation.

Step-grandparenting is not for the faint of heart! Yet, many of us will become step-grandparents. With patience, consistency, and time, step-grandparents can build loving, meaningful relationships with their step-grandchildren. This phenomenon and tips for step-grandparenting are discussed further in a separate section in this chapter.

Differing expectations and practices in other cultures

Different cultures may have widely different expectations of the role of grandparents. Japanese tradition, for example, suggests that the mother of the first-born son has a special position of influence in the household. In many African countries, traditionally grandmothers provide daily childcare so that daughters can go back to work or have more time to care for infants. It is important for everyone in a multicultural family to apply Principle One, that is, to speak up about their own expectations and wishes for the grandparenting role, and to accept that people's expectations may be different.

Cultural practices related to dress, manners, and privileges may also vary. Marion talked about her indignation when she learned that her granddaughter would wear a traditional hijab (head scarf) when she came of age, and of how she changed her mind about making a fuss over this.

I was furious when my daughter told me that she had agreed – at the request of her Muslim husband and his mother – to encourage her daughter to wear a hijab when she comes of age. Why should she wear what I saw as a symbol of forced silence and oppression? Then I heard an interview on the radio with a Canadian-born Muslim university student who has chosen to wear the head scarf because she finds it liberating. She said that wearing the hijab has given her freedom from the way Western society constantly judges young women on their attractiveness, hairstyle, makeup, and physical self. I remembered how I had struggled as a young woman to be recognized for who I was, not how I looked. I decided to say nothing and to wait and see how this will play out in a few years. Whatever decision my granddaughter makes, I will stand by her.

Concerns about prejudice and discrimination

Grandparents instinctively want to protect their children and grandchildren from prejudice and discrimination. Sam talks about his indignation at the way his son-in-law and grandchildren are treated, especially when they travel.

My daughter married a man from the Middle East. He and their children are often discriminated against, especially when they travel. The fear of terrorism has clouded the acceptance of the family, despite the fact that they are U.S. citizens with good jobs and no past involvement in any activities related to homeland security. I feel angry and helpless because I cannot protect them from this intolerance. Sometimes, I wish my daughter had chosen someone else, but then I look at my beautiful grandchildren and what a good father he is, and I know that they are right for each other.

Allan, a grandfather with three grandchildren whose parents are Caucasian and black, believes that racism within the family should be confronted immediately. When visiting in-laws made prejudiced remarks, he made himself perfectly clear.

> I told them I did not want to hear any talk about differences in colour or religion or anything else for that matter. I said that my grandchildren were just like them and if they wanted to play cards at my house they had better accept this.

Remaining neutral in times of conflict and family breakup

When a couple divorces, grandparents have a natural tendency to side with their child against his or her spouse. The best thing to do is to remain neutral. Your job is to be an unwavering advocate for your grandchild and to remain non-judgmental about the breakup. This is discussed further in the next section.

DEALING WITH DIVORCE OR SEPARATION

Today as many as one in every two children will experience a family breakup. This is a very difficult time for all concerned. Ironically, just at the time that children need their parents the most, they are least available for them, as the parents themselves try to deal with their own feelings and the many changes going on in their lives. Grandparents can help by providing a stable, caring, non-judgmental, and loving presence for their grandchildren and their adult children. Here are some specific ideas on how to be supportive:

Understand your grandchild's feelings. Most children of divorce or separation feel some degree of blame when their parents break up. They may think that if they had been better behaved, their parents might have stayed together. Most will go through the same stages of grief that affect adults in a loss – denial, anger or resentment, bargaining, depression, and finally acceptance. Your grandchild may be troubled by a sense of abandonment or rejection. Helping him cope with and understand these feelings can help him deal with the present and feel more positive about the future.

Anne describes how her granddaughter reacted to her parents' separation and how Anne handled things.

> During the breakup, Louise stayed at my house fairly often. She had a lot of nightmares and started to wet the bed again, after she had been dry all night for almost a year. I figured that these reactions were normal and would pass when she learned to accept the changes in her life. I held her a lot and told her it was no big deal to wet the bed once in a while. We talked about her nightmares and I stayed with her until she went back to sleep. We got a dream catcher for her bedroom at home to help stop the bad dreams from coming through. Sure enough, about three months later she was making it through the night again, and the nightmares were a lot less common.

Help your grandchild feel secure and loved. Tell her that you love her and that she does not need to fear losing you. Ask her parents if you can have a special scheduled time with her once a week (or more) if possible. However, if a recently separated in-law feels that weekly visits by the former spouse's parents are too difficult to manage for the moment, settle for a less-frequent schedule. Patience and flexibility will pay off in the long run. When you are with your grandchild, plan to spend time having fun. Praise her for doing well and trying hard. Show your love in every way you can; give her plenty of physical and emotional attention.

Do not take sides and do maintain positive relationships with both parents. While this may be the hardest action of all, it is likely the most important in terms of maintaining positive family relationships, according to the parents we talked with who had undergone a divorce.

Leslie, who went through a bitterly contested divorce, talks about how grandparents can help or make things worse in this situation.

My ex-husband is very close to his parents (especially his mother). When we split up, his parents immediately sided with their son. They bad-mouthed me in front of the children and refused to talk to me. This escalated the problems my ex and I had and made the divorce proceedings more drawn out. I understand that a parent's first loyalty is to his or her own child, and I suspect having someone to blame made them feel less guilty about their son's part in the breakup, but grandparents have tremendous potential to do good or to do bad. They need to rise above the conflict and remain neutral for the benefit of all, especially their grandchildren. My kids love their father and me, and they cannot understand their grand-parents' attitude toward me.

Help your adult children get through this hard time.
Some grandparents can mediate by gently helping the parents resolve conflicts in the divorce process that they were unable to work out when married. Or they can suggest that the couple go to a mediator or get support from community resources such as the Church or a family counselling centre. They should be steadfast in their love for the chil-dren and if possible take them out of the conflicted home to have quiet and fun times together. Since one or both parents becomes a single parent overnight, offering to babysit helps a lot. Grandparents also need to remain the keepers of the family traditions and memories. Children love this consistency and it helps them feel confident about who they are.

STEP-GRANDPARENTING
According to the Stepfamily Foundation (U.S.), one out of six chil-dren live in a stepfamily. You may "acquire" step-grandchildren when your children remarry (or marry a divorced person), or if you remarry yourself. In both these circumstances, grandparents have an opportunity to become a force for good, by sharing their love with children throughout a stressful situation.

Many boomers who remarried in their thirties and forties have lived with and raised both birth children and stepchildren as their own. They worry about being fair when it comes to grandchildren.

Betty had step-grandchildren first, although she would never have referred to them this way. They were her grandchildren and she loved them. In fact, she took secret pride that with four loving grandmothers, she had been the first to babysit each new grandchild. When her son announced they were expecting, Betty was surprised by some of her friends' reactions.

> I was asked by more than a few friends if I was excited about having my *own* grandchild. But I already considered the step-grandchildren as *mine*. I began to worry that my stepdaughter and her husband might think that I would become less interested and involved. I decided to make a concerted effort to show that there would be no difference once the new baby was born. At first I ran myself ragged trying to spend equal time with both sets of grandchildren. I was still working full-time in a demanding career. I finally realized that this was *my* problem. My stepdaughter and her husband were as excited about the new baby as I was, and they had no doubt that I was a loving grandmother to their three wonderful children.

Many factors affect the quality of the relationship between a step-grandparent and a step-grandchild. Some of these are the same for all grandchildren, including geographic and emotional availability, while other factors are unique to the situation of the extended family.

- The first factor is the step-grandchild's age at the time he enters your life. The older the child, the less likely that a step-grandparent will have a significant role in the child's life.
- The second factor is whether or not your step-grandchildren live

full-time with your adult child. If the children live mostly outside your extended family, you will see them less often.

- The third factor is how your grandchild feels about his parent's remarriage and the nature of his relationship with the step-parent. Obviously, if a child has a loving and trusting relationship with her new step-parent, she will be more open to a relationship with her step-grandparents.

- The fourth factor is how you feel about accepting step-grandchildren as your own. Step-grandparents who have the most meaningful relationships with their step-grandchildren never make reference to or think about them being "steps." They simply treat them the same as they do their biological grandchildren. This ideal scenario does not happen overnight. Studies show that most step-grandparents who go gently and are available, without asking for any reward or feedback (such as verbal declarations of the children's love and respect) can develop significant attachments and meaningful relationships.

Peggy and Jo became "instant" step-grandparents when their eldest daughter announced that she was committed to a man who had two children from a previous marriage, aged eight and ten. They jumped on a plane to Calgary as soon as they could to meet their daughter's new family.

We spent the first weekend with our new grandchildren becoming friends and getting to know one another. We followed this up with e-mails and letters. Six months later when they came to spend a week with us, Haley and Cooper asked if they could call me "Grandma." I almost cried I was so happy. From then on, I have always introduced them as my grandchildren. And though I have eight grandchildren in all, I make a special point of bragging about Haley, because so far she is my only granddaughter.

Real life in a stepfamily may not always be as smooth as it was for Peggy and Jo. Many children need time and support to adjust to the demands of getting to know and accept a step-parent, step-siblings, and step-grandparents. Here are some tips to help ease the transition.

Tips for Step-Grandparents

1. Be sensitive to existing grandparent-grandchild relationships and what is happening in the family. There might be jealousy or simply a lack of comfort with getting to know new relatives in a blended family. Aim to be an important and loving friend to your step-grandchildren and other family members.
2. Be sensitive to the impact of a family breakup on the children. Be a supportive listening post, especially for older grandchildren who are working through emotional issues related to the family breakup and remarriage. Never interfere in family dynamics.
3. Put your needs on hold for a while. You may be eager to become a "real" grandparent to your new grandchildren, and to secure the joy that comes with giving and receiving unconditional love, but the last thing a child needs is to be expected to have an instant relationship with step-grandparents.
4. Talk about your role. Make it clear to your step-grandchildren's parents and to older grandchildren that you are willing and want to be a grandparent, but clarify and discuss how you – and they – see your role.
5. Have fun with your step-grandchildren. You cannot buy their love or happiness but fun times break the tension, build happy memories, and help establish loving relationships.
6. Be steady, reliable, and patient. Healing takes time.

DIVORCE OR SEPARATION AND CHILD DEVELOPMENT

All children go through developmental behaviour changes, but children who experience divorce may exhibit more extremes in their behaviour during this stressful time. The following are guidelines for what you might encounter in your grandchildren at different ages and stages.

Birth to twelve months

Babies become irritable and hyperactive when parents are stressed. They may cry frequently and have sleep or digestive problems. Older infants are aware of the absence of a parent and are increasingly fearful of separation and strangers. Holding the baby securely and using a calm, soothing voice can help reassure the child. Attentive and consistent care by loving parents, grandparents, and other caregivers is important at this age. Bring along familiar blankets, bottles, toys, pacifiers, or a favourite stuffed animal. These can provide immense comfort and should accompany the child when he goes to a different house.

Toddlers

In times of stress, toddlers may regress to earlier stages of behaviour and can experience sleep problems and nightmares. They may cling to their parents and grandparents or express anger toward a parent. Provide consistent and loving attention. Recognize that, given time and support, old behaviours (such as thumb-sucking) will disappear and newly developed skills (such as toilet training) will reappear. Be patient and give stressed toddlers extra time to prepare for daily activities, such as dressing or going outside to play with Grandpa.

Preschoolers and early school-aged children

Children this age begin to understand that their parents do not love each other any more and that they will not be living together. They may believe and have rich fantasies about their parents getting back together. They are likely to blame themselves for the divorce, and may exhibit signs of worry, sadness, or anger. Repeatedly tell children that they are not responsible for the divorce and reassure them that they will be well taken care of. You can read books together about children and divorce and help them express themselves in non-verbal ways such as puppet shows or drawing and painting. Be sensitive to their fears and listen well. Express your concern for both parents and reassure the child that even though the family lives apart, all of you will continue to love him.

Preteens

Kids experiencing divorce at this age may feel cheated, hurt, guilty, and just plain mad! It is not unusual for preteens in this situation to act angry and pick fights. Offer activities to burn off steam, such as going swimming or painting or pottery as a way to express pent-up emotion in appropriate ways. Reassure them that they are not the cause of the divorce. Provide positive feedback and make them feel special and secure.

Adolescents

While teens are more likely to understand what divorce means, they may still blame themselves or have difficulty accepting the reality. They may withdraw from long-time friends and favourite activities or act out by avoiding family gatherings or acting sullen. Some may start to worry about adult matters, such as the family's financial security, and feel obligated to take on more adult responsibilities in the family. Maintain open lines of communication with your adolescent grand-children; reassure them of your love and continued involvement in their lives. Honour family rituals, such as holiday dinners or going to the hockey game together. Listen carefully but never use teenagers as confidants for how you feel about the breakup.

QUESTIONS AND ANSWERS

Q: My daughter and her husband are going through an "open adoption," which involves them meeting and staying in touch with the birth mother. We are terrified that the birth mother will change her mind or the child will not fully attach to his new family if the birth mother stays in contact. What can we do?

A: Most prospective adoptive parents and grandparents are haunted by the fear that the birth mother will want her baby back. In fact, less than 1 per cent of finalized adoptions are challenged legally. Open adoptions are a good idea because the mother is less likely to challenge the adoption if she has the opportunity to meet the new parents. Don't worry about your grandchild becoming attached to both the parents and you. This happens naturally with consistent, loving care on a day-to-day basis.

Q: My grandson who is eleven lives with his mother and her female life partner. He sees his father only occasionally. I am afraid that he does not have enough exposure to male role-models and I know he is being teased at school by some of the other boys. We live almost a thousand miles away from the family, but our son, who is heterosexual, lives in the same city as my grandson.

A: Virtually all unbiased research studies into same-sex parenting reveals that children in same-sex households develop normally. There are, however, anecdotal accounts of children having to endure ridicule and taunting from other youths because of their parents' sexual orientation. Since your son lives in the same city, he can serve as an important role model, male companion, and supporter of his nephew. Meanwhile, you can continue to express your unconditional love and respect for both your grandson and his parents. See Principle Eight for some ideas about doing this from a distance.

Q: My wife and I came from India and our children were born in Canada. Against our wishes, my son married a French-Canadian woman, instead of the bride from India that we proposed. We have come to love our daughter-in-law, especially since the births of our two grandchildren. We are unsure what to do about teaching our grandchildren about our beliefs, and how to involve this family in our traditional celebrations and rituals. My son says he does not care either way. My daughter-in-law is

open to mixing our cultures somewhat but the French-Canadian traditions are very important to her. Her parents, who live in Quebec, speak
little English and we speak no French.

A: Talk to your son and his wife and ask whether they have any objec-
tions to your teaching your grandchildren about your culture and
religion when they visit you. If they agree, engage the grandchildren in
those traditions that are most important to you. Encourage their
parents to participate. Make it fun and interesting and age-appropriate.
Help your grandchildren make things that they can use to explain some
of your traditions to their other grandparents, so they will feel included
or at least know what is happening. Ask your grandchildren and their
mother about French-Canadian traditions that the other grandparents
celebrate. You never know, there may even be parallels!

Q: My son and his wife divorced after an extended custody battle. My
daughter-in-law was given custody of the children. My son moved on
to a new relationship and rarely sees his daughter from his first marriage. We are very close to our granddaughter; in fact, we looked after
her during the day for several years while her parents were working. My
ex-daughter-in-law is denying us access to our granddaughter. She says
that she wants to sever all ties with our family. Do we have any legal
recourse to get to see our beloved granddaughter?

A: The legal pendulum has swung back and forth on this issue, especially since a high-profile case in 2000 when the U.S. Supreme Court
recognized the parents' rights as primary. In reality, visiting rights are
more a question of family dynamics than of legal rights. If you need to
resort to the courts to sort out who can see whom, you are already in
trouble. Try to remain calm and positive, and to come to some kind of
agreement with your daughter-in-law, even if it's only minimal at first.
Mediation is another option. A mediator is a neutral third party who
can help you and your daughter-in-law come to an agreement.

WHAT THE RESEARCH TELLS US

Grandchildren Love Their Step-Grandparents Too

Many grandchildren are as willing to accept a step-grandparent as vice versa. Researchers studied step-grandchildren's perceptions of their step-grandparents. Most of the children viewed their step-grandparent as someone they cared about and respected. Most maintained contact with their step-grandparent beyond high school; the majority wanted more contact with their step-grandparents; and almost half viewed their relationship with their step-grandparent as important, both personally and socially.

Source: Trygstad, D.W., and G.F. Sanders. "The Significance of Step-Grandparents," *International Journal of Aging and Human Development*, 29(2) (1989): 119-134.

Cohabitation Has Increased

In the U.S., the total number of unmarried, cohabiting heterosexual couples increased by more than ten times from 1960 to 2000: from 439,000 to 4.7 million couples. Among high-school students 66 per cent of men and 59 per cent of women "agree" or "mostly agree" that "It is usually a good idea for a couple to live together before getting married in order to find out whether they really get along."

Sources: U.S. Census Bureau, *Statistical Abstract of the United States: 2000.*

Bachman, J.G., L.D. Johnston, and P.M. O'Malley. *Monitoring the Future: Questionnaire Responses from the Nation's High School Seniors, 2000.* Ann Arbor, MI: Institute for Social Research, University of Michigan, 2001.

When Grandparents Divorce

A recent study showed that grandparents who divorce don't have as much contact with their grandkids, feel less close to them, and consider the role of grandparenting less important to their lives. This is especially true for grandfathers, who report much less contact with grandkids, fewer shared activities, and higher levels of conflict with their grandchildren than grandmothers who have divorced or grandparents who have not split up. Obviously, some grandparents who divorce remain just as close to their grandchildren as before. One's marital situation is just one of the factors in how and why families stay connected.

Source: Study by Valerie King at Pennsylvania State University, reported by Karen S. Peterson in *USA Today*, 2001.

THE LAST WORD

These following jewels were written or spoken by actual students and have not been retouched. They help to put our sometimes intense feelings about adoption and religion into perspective.

What It Means to Be Adopted

A group of first-graders were discussing a picture of a family. One little boy in the picture had different colour hair than the other family members. When one of the students suggested that he was adopted, a little girl said, "I know all about adoptions because I was adopted."

"What does it mean to be adopted?" asked another child.

"It means," said the girl, "that you grew in your mommy's heart instead of her tummy."

Bible Stories Retold by Students

When adults are as tolerant of different religious views as kids are, we can see the humour in the following bible stories, retold by students and uncorrected for spelling and grammar.

"Moses led the Hebrews to the Red Sea, where they made unleavened bread, which is bread made without any ingredients. The Egyptians were all drowned in the dessert. Afterwards, Moses went up on Mount Cyanide to get the Ten Amendments. The Fifth Commandment is to humour thy father and mother. The Seventh Commandment is thou shalt not admit adultery."

"David was a Hebrew king skilled at playing the liar. He fought with the Finklesteins, a race of people who lived in Biblical times. Solomon, one of David's sons, had three hundred wives and seven hundred porcupines."

"The people who followed the Lord were called the twelve decibels. The epistles were the wives of the apostles. One of the opossums was St. Matthew who was by profession of a taximan."

Be Accepting, Empathetic, and Positive

Nobody can do for little children what grandparents do. Grand-parents sort of sprinkle stardust over the lives of little children.

— Alex Haley

In your childhood and teenage years, who were your biggest fans? Who provided you with unconditional love and acceptance? Who encouraged you and had confidence in your abilities? If you are lucky, your mother and father played this role. For others, it may also have been a teacher, a coach, or another family member. Regardless, the importance of having caring adults in *your* corner when you are growing up cannot be underestimated. This chapter is based on the assumption that grandparents have the opportunity to contribute to the long-term health and happiness of our grandchildren by being an active member of their fan club.

Principle Five is about being an accepting, empathetic, and positive fan. This principle comes naturally to most grandparents. Many of us love the very idea of being a grandparent, long before it is even a reality. And when the first grandchild is born, the love affair begins. Relieved of the day-to-day responsibilities of parenting, we find it easier to give focused, loving attention to our grandchildren. We can overlook bad behaviour or developmental lags because they don't reflect on our parenting skills. We can relax and enjoy our grandchildren's enthusiasm and energy, and can then go back to our everyday lives and recharge our batteries.

As grandparents, we have earned the right to stand back and simply enjoy the time we spend with our grandchildren. But we need to be aware that in our interactions with our grandchildren, we are giving them clear messages, both consciously or unconsciously. We do this through the behaviours and attitudes we model and encourage or discourage in them. The intent of this chapter is to make us more aware of the potential impact of our behaviours and attitudes on our grandchildren, especially for those lucky grandparents who see their grandchildren frequently.

THEN AND NOW
Grandparent as "fan" is not a new concept. Our stereotypical image of the ideal grandparent has always been a warm, nurturing figure who loves unconditionally and inspires with his or her wisdom. Grandparents through the ages have approached their role with an open mind, an open heart, and a positive attitude. What is new is the body of research on child development that supports this principle, particularly in the areas of resilience, optimism, and emotional intelligence in children.

In the early seventies, many of us used behaviour modification theories and practices with our children: rewarding good behaviour, ignoring inappropriate behaviour, and when necessary, punishing bad or dangerous behaviour in our children. We were told to let our children suffer the natural consequences of their actions, unless of course this was dangerous to their health. There were fewer books available on child rearing and even fewer reports on child development research in the popular press.

In the eighties, cognitive psychology began to influence parenting practices. Child-development specialists encouraged us to develop self-esteem in our children. We were urged to engage in open discussion so that our children would become insightful and self-motivated to change and grow. We struggled to balance being more liberal in our practices as parents, with maintaining some semblance of control.

In the nineties, many of our children had left home and we heaved a collective sigh of relief. Perhaps too soon – some of those grown-up children returned to the nest. Nevertheless, we no longer sought out books on child rearing. In the interim, the market became flooded with books, Web sites, and magazines that provide excellent advice on parenting. Much of the information they contain is based on research in the areas of emotional intelligence, optimism, and resilience in children.

Although we now have ample evidence to support the importance of being accepting, empathetic, and positive with children, the current environment makes this challenging for parents and teachers alike. The world in which we live is perceived as more dangerous and threatening. Our grandchildren are bombarded with images of war, violence, and death. They are taught to avoid and fear strangers. As a result, modern parents have a tough job ahead of them: how to raise resilient, optimistic, and emotionally intelligent children within the constraints of the modern world. As boomer grandparents, we can contribute to the development of these traits in our grandchildren by being among their biggest fans. Armed with more information on child development than earlier generations, we can find ways to use this knowledge to enrich our everyday experience with our grandchildren.

GRANDPARENTS AS FANS

Many of the parents and grandparents we talked with have warm, loving memories of their own grandparents. Mary Jane recalls being at a family camp with her children and grandchildren recently, discussing the writing of this book with a few other campers.

One young mother, overhearing the conversation, came over and said: "Oh, let me tell you about my grandmother, she was the most wonderful person in my life. She was my biggest fan. My grandmother was warm and caring and interested in everything I did. She was also kind and smart. My first child was actually born on her birthday. Unfortunately, she died before I had children and this was the one thing she always said she wanted to live to see."

When I then asked about her own children's grandparents, there was silence. With a sad face, she said quietly, "My parents and my husband's parents just aren't interested and I feel so sad for my children. No one can give them the same kind of love and acceptance as grandparents, and they will never experience that."

While grandparents can never replace parents (except when grandparents are actually raising their grandchildren), we can be a positive force in their lives. With increases in divorce, separation, and single-parenting, our grandchildren need us more than ever.

Accepting Our Grandchildren

In his research on developing resilience in children, author and psychologist Robert Brooks talks about the importance of accepting children for who they are, not necessarily for who we want them to be. Children differ in many ways, including their physical features, their motor skills and intellectual abilities, and their temperaments. (We are all born with a certain temperament. Principle Seven: Be Consistent, Reliable, and Fair talks further about temperament and its influence on how children develop.)

Resilient children that feel accepted for who they are, also feel secure in reaching out to others, in seeking support, and in learning how to solve problems. They are more likely to understand what they can change in their lives and how to manage mistakes and failures. They are also more willing to take appropriate risks.

Accepting our grandchildren for who they are is easy when they conform more or less to our expectations. But when they are not as well-behaved as we would like, or when they do not show an interest or aptitude for family activities, or when their demeanour or manners leave something to be desired, our challenge begins. Martha describes how she felt and reacted when her father was having a hard time accepting her five-year-old son, Darcy.

> Dad was in the military and was never one to show much emotion. He is pretty good with the girls but he thinks boys should be tough or they will turn into sissies. Darcy is very bright and sensitive. He is also quite timid and even most children's movies scare him. He loves to read and go to the science museum. We knew Dad loved Darcy but he was always teasing him about not liking sports and of being afraid of his own shadow. One day, Darcy burst into tears and said he didn't want his grandpa to come over because he made him feel bad. We were devastated and knew that Dad would be too – but we had to deal with it. We were diplomatic but firm. Dad was a bit defensive at first but we stressed how accepting he was of the same behaviour in the girls and how they loved to spend time with him. We encouraged Dad to take Darcy to the library and the technology museum. It has been interesting to watch Dad change, as well as his relationship with all three kids. Even the girls seem to enjoy him more because he has begun to ask them what they would like to do. The irony is that Dad and Darcy now have a common interest – airplanes!

Accepting each grandchild's uniqueness means not playing favourites (see Principle Seven). It also means that we need to get to know them, their likes and dislikes, their strengths and weaknesses. Becoming acquainted with our grandchildren is an enjoyable activity but not always convenient or easy.

Myrna and Norm have ten grandchildren scattered across Canada. They range in age from three to thirteen and naturally have different interests and skills. These energetic grandboomers have high-profile professional careers but have made it a priority to get to know and appreciate the uniqueness of each grandchild.

Our grandchildren are all terrific. Each child has a special gift. We try and find the things that make them feel good about themselves; for example, our oldest grandchild is very bright and an excellent student but not really interested in sports. He is, however, a keen and excellent skier, so that is an activity we do together. We focus on the things that our grandchildren do well. We have always praised them, even from an early age.

By accepting our grandchildren and building on their existing strengths, we are helping them develop the skills that will make them more resilient. Many of today's child-development experts feel that in the past, we spent too much time trying to "fix" our children's problems rather than building on their abilities. Being a fan is about understanding and embracing the uniqueness of each of our grandchildren.

Showing Empathy Towards Our Grandchildren

Empathy is the foundation of any good relationship. It is about putting yourself in someone else's shoes and trying to see the world from their perspective. Being empathetic with your grandchildren doesn't imply that you agree with everything they do. It does mean, however, that you try to understand and appreciate their point of view. It is easier to be empathetic when our grandchildren do what we ask them to do, are successful in their activities, and are warm and responsive. Unfortunately, this will not always be the case. Ruth talks about the time her fifteen-year-old granddaughter came to visit with purple hair.

I am conservative by nature. I was always thankful that my three children didn't go for the punk look when they were young. And here is my beautiful granddaughter Melissa looking like a street kid. My first reaction was to want to ask "What have you done?" Thank goodness I didn't. I just smiled and said that I was so happy to see her, which was true. Melissa eventually asked me what I thought of her hair. I didn't want to lie so I said that while I loved the colour purple, I would probably never dye my own hair that colour. She laughed and we talked about how she loves having purple hair and what other colours she would like to try. Melissa is a bright, caring person and I love our relationship. I think she knows that I would prefer her hair its natural colour but she also knows that I love her unconditionally, and that I am always interested in her life.

On occasion empathy simply means being sensitive to the idiosyncrasies of our grandchildren. Some grandchildren are outgoing and love to be the centre of attention, while others are mortified by being singled out, especially in front of others. One grandmother with a wonderful sense of humour learned that her new step-granddaughter had little experience with light-hearted adults. Instead of laughing at Grandma's jokes about being interested in boys now that she was thirteen, her granddaughter became upset and embarrassed.

I quickly learned to never ask questions of or make comments about my granddaughter in front of others. By scheduling outings one-on-one, we eventually developed a comfortable relationship, if more formal than I would have liked. This whole experience has been good for me. I have learned to slow down and pay more attention to all my grandchildren. I have re-evaluated my assumptions that they are all alike. Now I am more in tune with them all – or at least try to be!

As grandparents, we have a unique opportunity to model an empathetic approach to people in general, not just our grandchildren, and to encourage this behaviour in them. We demonstrate empathy when we are accepting and respectful of others. Being around people who are critical is depressing at the best of times but when grandparents and significant others are critical around children, this can have long-lasting repercussions.

·Children who experience empathy are more likely to be empathetic themselves. They will be more tolerant of others and see mistakes as an opportunity for learning. This helps build a resilient mindset in which they are better able to accept and overcome their own shortcomings. It also increases their ability to get along well with others. Empathy is one of the building blocks for our grandchildren to become responsible, caring, and productive adults.

Being Positive with Our Grandchildren

Grandparents who are positive and enthusiastic are more fun to spend time with. They are also teaching their grandchildren the attitudes and skills of optimism – what a wonderful gift! Optimistic children have an edge over others: they see life as full of options and opportunities over which they have some control. They are more likely to try and find solutions to problems because they have a tendency to believe that there is always realistic hope, no matter how bad things get. Pessimistic children feel they have little control over events so are more likely to give up easily. Fiona could see the difference in her two grandchildren at an early age.

Sienna is enthusiastic about everything: school, soccer, gymnastics, piano lessons, friendships. Things don't always go smoothly for her. Sometimes her friends are mean. She isn't a very skilled soccer player and this year she wasn't picked for the school concert. But nothing seems to get her down for long. She will talk about her problems and disappointments and she always seems to be able to put things in perspective. She knows she has lots of other friends and that she may not be good at soccer but she is great at gymnastics. She expects things to turn out well and they generally do.

Her cousin Tim often has a different perspective. It's harder for him to be positive. For example, he is one of the better players on his baseball team, but he attributes this to his being bigger, not more skilled. He has a few good school friends according to his teacher, but at home he worries a lot about fitting in. He has a tendency to give up when things don't come easily and naturally.

How can grandparents help their grandchildren be more optimistic? They can do so by being optimistic themselves:

- By putting problems in perspective
- By modelling good problem solving
- By helping grandchildren see their problems as temporary and solvable
- By helping grandchildren accomplish something

Success breeds optimism. Some grandparents seem to know intuitively how to encourage and instill confidence in their grandchildren. Others miss golden opportunities, despite their best intentions. One young father recounts how his dad decided one day that he would build a toy-box for his grandson Tanner. While the act was motivated by love, his father lost a chance to build a closer relationship with Tanner and to teach him some new skills. This was because Tanner was not allowed to help. He could only watch.

Granddad Dick, on the other hand, describes how he noticed that his young grandson always tagged along whenever he was working around the house.

I decided that I would teach Patrick how to use some basic tools, just like my dad taught me. So I bought him his own tool kit. Now whenever I get out a hammer, there is Patrick, hammer in hand, wanting to help. He's actually not bad for a three-year-old.

While optimism has a genetic component, it is also a habit that can be learned at any age, grandparents included. Indeed, developing the habits of optimism will benefit us as much as our grandchildren. Optimistic adults tend to be healthier and live longer. So get out those rose-coloured glasses!

SOME BARRIERS TO BEING ACCEPTING, EMPATHETIC, AND POSITIVE WITH OUR GRANDCHILDREN

Even for grandparents who are accepting, empathetic, and positive by nature, there are times when it is difficult to put this principle into practice. The grandparents we talked with discussed some of their challenges.

Some grandchildren are easier to get along with than others. Some have behavioural or emotional problems. Others are just so very different from us in terms of temperament and interests that we don't bond as naturally and effortlessly. Some grandparents inherit step-grandchildren who may be older, wounded by divorce or separation, or simply uninterested in developing a relationship with their step-grandparents.

Karen was excited about having grandchildren when her only son married a widow with two young children. Her step-granddaughter was five, bright and good-natured. Her step-grandson was seven, active and talkative. It soon became clear that he was also difficult to handle.

> I tried to treat both grandchildren the same, but Todd was driving me crazy. He was like a whirling dervish. I found myself impatient and unwilling to babysit. I was beginning to almost dislike him. Then the school suggested he be tested. As a result, he was put on medication and that calmed him down considerably. He became much easier to handle. I am now able to enjoy his company. He is still active and has a shorter attention span than Sarah, but we are becoming very close. We bike and hike and I am even teaching him how to ski. I feel bad that I was so impatient at first but I knew little about hyperactive children. Now, even if he has a bad day, I am able to adjust to his energy level.

Unfortunately, there isn't always a magic bullet that will turn all our grandchildren into easy-to-relate-to children. There is, however, abundant literature available to help modern grandparents deal with special children. It is up to each of us to decide how much effort we are willing and able to invest in these relationships. We also need to keep in mind that these are the children who could perhaps benefit most from having loving fans. They need grandparents who accept and understand them, and who help them feel positive about themselves and optimistic about their future.

A belief that we shouldn't shield children from the harsh realities of life. Some of us grew up to believe that encouraging a positive attitude would do our children no favours. It would leave them unprepared to cope with life's ups and downs. Now we know it is quite the opposite. Being optimistic is not about being an unrealistic Pollyanna. Optimism is a problem only if taken to an extreme that may lead children to put themselves at risk by underestimating a real danger.

SUGGESTIONS FOR ĐEVELOPING
A GOOD RELATIONSHIP WITH YOUR GRANDCHILD
Adapted from *Being A GRAND Parent* by H.G. Lingren

1. Listen to your grandchildren. By tuning in to them, you may be able to tune out some of your own problems.
2. Talk with your grandchildren. Keep these tips in mind:

   - Get to the point and stick to it without rambling or repeating.
   - Talk about lively and interesting subjects.
   - Avoid complaints. Stay away from such subjects as health and minor everyday gripes.
   - Avoid concentrating on I, I, I, or me, me, me. Do NOT monopolize the conversation.

- Maintain eye contact to determine if your grandchild is really hearing what you say or is bored.
- Be enthusiastic and excited about what is being said.

3. Express your feelings. Laugh when you are happy and cry when you are sad.
4. Be aware of your own prejudices and unresolved issues.
5. Be aware of the example you are setting, because your grand-children and your children will learn much about love from seeing and feeling it.

RESILIENCE, EMPATHY, OPTIMISM AND CHILD DEVELOPMENT

Resilience

The ability to cope with and overcome adversity is considered by some child psychologists to be one of the most important skills that every child needs. Resilient children deal more effectively with stress and pressure. They cope better with everyday challenges and are likely to bounce back from disappointment, adversity, and trauma. They are also better at goal setting, problem solving, and relating with others than children with low resilience.

Empathy

Empathy normally develops in the first six years of a child's life. It is seen in most babies when they respond to another crying infant, turning their head towards the crying baby and frequently crying themselves. According to Lawrence Shapiro, a psychotherapist and expert in emotional intelligence, children enter a second stage of empathy between the ages of one and two. They begin to recognize that another's distress is not their own. By age six, most children have the ability to see things from another's perspective and act accordingly some of the time. In late childhood, between the ages of ten and twelve, children develop abstract empathy, a concern for people they don't know such as those who live in other countries or who are disadvantaged.

Although some children seem to be naturally more empathetic than others, there are many things that parents and significant others can do to develop and nourish empathy in children, besides being empathetic themselves. Shapiro suggests that we can "raise the bar" on our expectations for considerate and responsible behaviour in children. Since experience is the best teacher, he also suggests that we practice random acts of kindness and involve our children and grandchildren in community service. Shapiro says:

> Children who are empathetic tend to be less aggressive and are more likely to be sharing and helpful. As a result they are better liked by those around them and are more successful in school and at work. It is not surprising that empathetic children become adults who have a greater capacity for intimacy and better relationships with their spouses, friends, and children.

Optimism

Studies suggest that developing the skills of optimism in children not only reduces the risk of depression, but also improves school performance, physical health, and the ability to handle disappointments and setbacks.

According to author Martin Seligman, optimism comes from realistic thinking combined with opportunities to meet and master age-appropriate challenges. Most young children feel omnipotent and are unrealistically optimistic until about age seven. After age seven, three factors influence their optimism: their primary caregiver's level of optimism (most often the mother), the form of criticism they hear when they fail, and the type of early losses and traumas they experience. If the latter are permanent and pervasive, children are more likely to become pessimistic and depressed.

QUESTIONS AND ANSWERS

Q: How can we tell my daughter and her husband that their frequent criticisms of their son Marley, are having a negative effect on his self-esteem? Marley is more interested in books and computers than his brothers, who are more interested in sports. The family has always teased him for being a "nerd" and liking school. He's now ten and refuses to talk about school and seems to want to hide his intelligence.

A: Unfortunately for Marley, his family seems to value achievement on the field more than in the classroom. It could also be that his parents are trying to compensate for the other children's lower intellectual ability by downplaying Marley's academic achievements. Nevertheless, both Marley and his brothers have talents that need to be recognized and areas where they need encouragement to develop further.

If your relationship with Marley's parents is an open one, you could approach them more in a coaching fashion than a telling one. You could say that you have noticed a change in Marley and describe what you have observed, and ask if they have noticed it also. You could ask if they have any idea why this might be happening. If the parents engage in this conversation, then you might suggest ways that you as grandparents could help Marley understand that being intelligent and doing well in school is a positive thing.

Regardless of your ability to discuss the issue with Marley's parents, you can find ways to encourage and engage Marley in areas and subjects that are of interest to him, either by sharing reading material, participating in related events, or even better, by finding ways to also engage his brothers' interest in the topics.

Q: My son has recently married a woman with two teenage girls. They are quiet and sullen and don't seem to want to get to know us. These are our first grandchildren. Any suggestions?

A: Your grandchildren could be acting this way because they are shy, nervous, or anxious. The easiest way to engage most people is to find their area of interest and be interested in the topic yourself. Ask your new granddaughters questions without being intrusive. Ask their mother what interests them. Perhaps you could find ways to do things one-on-one in their areas of interest, even if this means shopping! By accepting them the way they are (quiet), by being interested in what interests them (even if it is hip-hop music), and by encouraging and acknowledging them, you will hopefully build trust and establish a relationship. It probably won't happen overnight.

WHAT THE RESEARCH TELLS US

Empty Praise Does Not Build Self-esteem

Child psychologists now suggest that self-esteem is only beneficial if it is a by-product of doing something well. They encourage parents and significant others, such as teachers and grandparents, to encourage mastery and skill building in children. Self-esteem will follow. Telling children they are wonderful and talented without any evidence does not build self-esteem. Encouraging them and providing opportunities for skill development does.

Source: Brooks, R., and S. Goldstein. *Raising Resilient Children*. New York: Contemporary Books, 2001.

The Importance of Secure Attachment

The literature on healthy child development has repeatedly shown the importance of "secure attachment" in promoting well-being, not only in infancy, but also in healthy adjustment during adolescence. Attachment is the emotional connection between two people. Life's first attachments are by far the most important, as they set a template for all later relationships. Experts suggest that "tuning in" to a baby's signals is key to building secure attachments. For example, sensitive parents and grandparents respond quickly and affectionately to crying. They also respond in different ways, depending on how a baby is crying. As children grow older, building on the early attachment years remains essential. Children and adolescents sense an emotional connection when their parents and grandparents empathize with their feelings, and provide an environment that is consistent, predictable, and loving.

Source: Steinhauer, P., M.D. "Raising a Healthy Child Depends on Time and Timing," *Transition,* June 1997.

Feeling Connected and Adolescent Behaviour

Feeling connected means feeling cared for, welcomed, and treated fairly. Empirical studies have shown that feeling connected at home and feeling connected at school are two of the most powerful determinants of which adolescents will stay out of such troubles as severe emotional stress, depression, drug or alcohol abuse, violent behaviour, dropping out of school, or unwanted pregnancy. Students who feel connected also tend to get better grades.

Source: National Longitudinal Study of Adolescent Health (U.S.), as reported in the *Journal of the American Medical Association,* September 10, 1997.

THE LAST WORD

Stories from Grandparents about Grandchildren

"I didn't know if my granddaughter had learned her colours yet, so I decided to test her. I would point out something and ask what colour it was. She would tell me and she was always correct. But it was fun for me, so I continued. At last, she headed for the door, saying sagely, 'Grandma, I think you should try to figure out some of these yourself!'"

A seven-year-old grandson surprised his grandmother one morning – he had made her coffee. She drank what was the worst cup of coffee in her life. When she got to the bottom, there were three of those little green army men in the cup. She said, "Honey, what are these army men doing in my coffee?" Her grandson said, "Grandma, it says on TV 'The best part of waking up is soldiers in your cup!'"

A three-year-old boy went with his granddad to see a new litter of kittens. On returning home, he breathlessly informed his grandmother, "There were two boy kittens and two girl kittens." "How did you know that?" his grandmother asked. "Grampa picked them up and looked underneath," he replied. "I think it's printed on the bottom."

"One summer evening during a violent thunderstorm I was tucking my small grandson into bed. I was about to turn off the light when he asked with a tremor in his voice, 'Grandma, will you sleep with me tonight?' I smiled and gave him a reassuring hug. 'I can't, dear,' I said. 'I have to sleep in Grandpa's room.' 'The big sissy,' he replied."

One Canadian grandmother phoned her grandson Travis after his first few days at kindergarten. She asked him what he had learned in school. He replied, "We learned the hockey song." She said, "The hockey song? How does that go?" Travis said, "Oh Grandma, you know the one, it starts like this – 'O Canada . . .'"

Be Playful and Spontaneous

Slow. Grandparents at Play.
— Sign in a Florida mobile-home park

There are many good reasons to be a playful and spontaneous grandparent. First and foremost, it is good for our grandchildren. Play is serious business for children. It helps them learn about ideas, language, problem solving, and relationships. Through play, children develop skills, imagination, and confidence, and find ways to express their emotions. Secondly, it strengthens our relationship with them, and makes the times we spend together more fun and joyful. And, if that isn't enough to convince you, consider this: playfulness and laughter are good medicine for aging adults. Think of it as internal jogging. There is ample evidence that humour, spontaneity, and play can help us live longer, healthier, and happier lives.

The young parents we talked with believe that playing with their children is one of the important ways that grandparents can support the family. Melanie suggested that grandparents share their experience and interest in things like gardening. Other young parents told us how their children look forward to visits with Grandpa or Grandma because they play special games and do activities together. Grandchildren also see playing as an important role. When asked what kind of things they like to do with their grandparents, fishing, swimming, going to the park, and playing cards were mentioned often.

As grandparents, we have several advantages over parents. We don't have to play peek-a-boo, tag, Barbies, or Monopoly every day. We don't have the same time-constraints as parents who run a household, work in and outside the home, and look after children twenty-four hours a day, seven days a week. With a little planning, we can find the time to play with our grandchild at some point in a visit.

Most grandboomers are healthy enough to participate in active play. In fact, a recent survey by the American Association of Retired Persons (AARP) found that the majority of grandfathers participated in exercise and sports with their grandchildren (from 75 per cent among those aged forty-five to forty-nine, to 67 per cent among those aged eighty-plus). Over 50 per cent of grandmothers also engaged in some form of physical activity with their grandchildren from time to time.

However, we "older folk" are not expected to roughhouse on the floor for an hour, or spike the volleyball, or perform a high dive (although some of us can and this impresses grandchildren immensely). Grandkids are happy to have us lie on the floor and cuddle, to cheer when they spike the ball, and to play judge by assigning them a score when they jump off the diving board. For all these reasons, we grandparents have a unique opportunity to use play (both active and quiet) as a way to have fun, to connect with our grandchildren, and to assist in their healthy development.

This chapter recognizes the value of play and introduces the idea of "playful grandparenting" – choosing to join children in their world, sometimes by literally getting down on the floor with them. Once you decide to be a playful grandparent, the rest is easy. You choose how you want to be engaged – playing peek-a-boo with an infant, sharing a bedtime story, helping your granddaughter land her first fish, applauding your grandson's puppet play, or joining in by taking on the role of the dastardly villain.

THEN AND NOW

The boomers, more than any other generation, were raised in an environment that supported our natural need to play. We were the doted-on offspring of hard-working, war-weary parents. Most of us had the chance to take swimming lessons and skate on outdoor rinks. Walking to school, riding our bicycles, and playing outside gave us the daily exercise we needed to stay relatively fit and lean. On Saturdays, we would leave home in the morning and play outside all day, as long as we were back when the streetlights came on.

Things are different for many of our grandchildren. Children don't play outside as much any more because of society's heightened sense of danger. Polls show that both Americans and Canadians feel that the threat to their physical safety is increasing, even though statistics show that the actual rates of violent crimes have dropped in recent years. As a result, children get driven to school and are more likely to play video games or surf the Net than play tag or kick the can. To a large extent spontaneous play has been replaced by organized activities. Pickup baseball has turned into competitive leagues and the go-carts we built out of scraps have been largely replaced by expensive, organized BMX racing. Psychologists warn that today's children are over-programmed and too busy for their own good. Youngsters rush from school to music lessons, gymnastics, Scouts, and swimming. Their parents spend two to three hours a week ferrying them about.

In trying to provide our children with structured activities and to protect them from the dangers of the world, we may be jeopardizing them in other ways. Children and young people learn about themselves and others through active play. It allows them to let off steam and angry feelings, and to stay in shape. Today, childhood obesity and inactivity are on the rise, as are behavioural problems and mental health issues among children and youth. Parents have been arrested for accosting the coach at a child's hockey game and children are dropping out of organized sport because it ceases to be fun, or their parents cannot afford the high registration fees. One wonders if bringing back the freedom of active, unorganized play would solve some of these problems.

However, wishing for the past and criticizing the present is not the answer. Grandboomers need to recognize and respect parents' concerns. We need to be vigilant about ensuring both the physical and emotional safety of our grandchildren when they are in our care. At the same time, we can experience the joy of sharing laughter, mastery, and wonderment when we play with our grandchildren.

PLAYFUL GRANDPARENTING

Playful grandparenting is not just about games, toys, and parties. It is also about having a sense of playfulness inside (some people call it the child within). When we giggle, sing a silly song, pretend to be a fish, make a thumb disappear, get into a pillow fight, or play dress-up with our grandchildren, we are rediscovering and sharing the child's spirit within us. And it feels wonderful!

Some of the grandboomers we talked to felt lukewarm, even anxious about this principle. One man said, "My wife does not hesitate to get down on the floor with the kids. I am not quite ready to do that." One grandmother said, "I'm prepared to work hard at being a good grandparent who gives and receives love and respect. But I am not prepared to act like a goof or play in the mud. That's a job for their parents and younger friends."

The funny thing is that when most grandparents who feel this way find themselves alone with their infant or toddler grandchild, their childlike imagination and sense of wonder kicks back in. They find themselves using baby talk, singing, blowing bubbles, and wondering how this tiny miracle sees the world. If we allow ourselves to relax and enjoy these kinds of activities, it is only a small step further to play store or build a fort or make up an adventure story. We've earned the right to let go of societal expectations that say we have to be dignified and efficient and work-oriented. And even if we do feel a little embarrassed pretending to be a prince or an alien monster, our grandkids aren't going to tell on us.

WHAT GETS IN THE WAY OF PLAY AND SPONTANEITY?

Inevitably, when fifty-eight-year-old Doug is having fun with his grandchildren, someone calls him "the biggest kid in the group." Doug is a natural at playful grandparenting. But this kind of behaviour does not come easily to all grandparents. Sometimes we hesitate to get involved, because the play is too rough or too silly or because we have other things we just *have* to do first. Sometimes when we join in, we feel bored, tired, distracted, or annoyed if the children cheat or cry. These feelings get in the way of our ability to relax, pay attention to our grandchildren's needs, and respond in a playful and spontaneous way.

Here are some ideas from grandboomers we interviewed on how to deal with some of the barriers to playful grandparenting:

The mess drives me crazy.
When kids grow up and leave, your home takes on more order and tidiness. It is easy to forget what it is like to have toys spread everywhere, and the mess that is created when kids come in from playing outside or help you make sugar cookies. Dorothy, a tidy housekeeper who likes things in their place, explains how she overcame her frustrations.

> At first I ran around trying to clean up after them as they played. This was frustrating, tiring, and no fun at all. Finally I decided to set some limits and live with the mess until they went home. My rules are pretty simple: shoes off when you enter the house, no destructive play like throwing toys around, cleaning up together as we bake, one five-minute blitz together to put away the toys before they leave or go to bed. I also decided to get organized ahead of time and to participate in the mess-making. So if crafts are on the agenda, I put newspaper down and get all the material ready ahead of time. I make sure the markers and paints are washable. Then I can do it with them and comment on how artistic they are, not on how much mess they are making. Since we live by the river I ask their moms to bring their rubber boots. I put on mine and we go

out to feed the ducks and explore. We leave all our boots by the door and just hose them down before we go in.

I can't wrestle or play tag any more. I'm out of shape. I have a bad back. I'm too tired.

Most young children love physical play, and "roughhousing" can be cathartic and connecting as long as the adult is sensitive to the child's safety and personal strength. Most granddads, in particular, love to throw kids in the air, and play chase and catch. But what happens when you really can't engage in this kind of play any more? Jason, an ex-athlete who developed a back problem in his fifties, explains how he handles the situation.

> My grandkids Madison and Jeff love to roughhouse after a meal. Now that I can't wrestle on the floor with them any more, we invented a new game. I sit on the big sofa and they take turns jumping up beside me. I grab them in a bear hug. Then I give them a trick to do (such as a somersault or five star-jumps) as a condition of releasing them from the hug. It's a little hard on the sofa but my back is feeling fine!

I can't afford costly toys and books or to take my grandchildren on expensive vacations.

If you think back to the times you spent with your own grandparents, it was likely the everyday, inexpensive things you did together that meant the most. Things like building a snowman, playing hide-and-seek, playing checkers, building a fence, taking hikes in the fall, or walking the dog, and stopping for ice cream.

Here are some other suggestions from grandboomers about inexpensive but effective ways to play with your grandchildren:

• Take your grandchildren to the library as soon as they are toddlers. When they are old enough, get them their own card with their name on it. Borrow books to read at your place or theirs and/or stay for storytime provided by your local librarian.

- Take them to local garage sales and allow them to buy inexpensive second-hand toys to keep at your house.
- Give babies and toddlers household objects to play with such as pots and pans, wooden spoons, and plastic measuring cups.
- Save egg cartons, shoeboxes, coffee cans, greeting cards, wrapping paper tubes, and other disposable items. Add some masking tape, glue, and markers. You'll be amazed at how they will turn these items into toys and artistic creations.
- Invest in a few good age-appropriate board games (second-hand is fine) and a deck of cards.
- Take grandkids to free activities in your neighbourhood (e.g., local carnivals) and to museums, arenas, and swimming pools on "free" days (many have one free day a week).
- Take them to movie matinees, which are usually half the price.
- Pack a picnic when you go on outings to avoid the cost (and heartburn) of a fast-food lunch.
- Consider an overnight camping holiday. It is inexpensive, there are loads of things for kids to do, and it provides a wonderful opportunity for you to enjoy and learn about nature together.

HOW TO BE THE PERFECT PLAYMATE

Children's play can be quiet, noisy, or in-between. It can be solo or involve other people. It can be spontaneous or organized. The trick is to be ready for all kinds of play, and to strike a balance between spontaneous play and activities that require some organization and leadership on your part. Usually, if you have the materials on hand, your grandchildren will let you know what and how they want to play. This doesn't mean you have to relinquish total control. You can make suggestions or designate some times as quiet play, when you or your grandchildren or both of you need some downtime.

Playful grandparents create environments that encourage all kinds of play. They give their grandchildren the lead and join in the fun in a way that builds confidence, trust, co-operation, and connections.

Enjoy creative play, including arts and crafts (e.g., painting, drawing, collage), music, singing and dancing. As you explore these activities, you will inevitably find that each grandchild has particular strengths and likes. Pablo Picasso said: "Every child is an artist. The problem is how to remain an artist once he grows up." Resist the urge to insist that your grandchild colour a tree green or build a house that has a roof. They will encounter enough critics in life. Our job is to encourage their creativity and praise their efforts.

Promote imaginary and dramatic play that allows children to try out different kinds of life roles, activities, and occupations, such as firefighter, actor, mother, father, astronaut, dancer, singer, farmer, doctor, nurse, soldier, etc. Dress-up clothes, old makeup and jewellery, occupational props, puppets, toy animals, bathtub toys, sandboxes, trucks, building materials, dolls, old microphones, telephones, and action figures encourage this kind of play. Remember the Tickle Trunk!

Be prepared to watch, applaud, and photograph your grandkids' "shows" and to participate in a role if they want you to. Don't be afraid to sing, even if you can't carry a tune. Singing soothes a fussy baby and delights a toddler. It invites school-aged children to make up their own verses and helps teens relax in the car. As long as the windows are up so no one else can hear you, teenage grandchildren are usually happy to sing along to Bob Marley or Elvis as you cruise down the highway.

Storytelling is an art that any grandparent can learn. And when you establish storytelling as a fun thing to do, inevitably your grandkids will want to join in. When Peggy and Jo are away with grandchildren in the summer, Grampa Jo starts a bedtime story that continues all week.

Jo involves the kids by making each of them a central character in the story. He asks them to supply the name of a city, an animal, a sport, a mode of transportation, a body part, and something scary. He then begins an outrageous story that eventually includes all of these items. There is a new chapter every night and the kids fall over themselves reminding him of what happened the night before (he almost always forgets the details). They howl over some of the corny, racy, and supposed-to-be-scary things that happen in the story, but they always come back for more.

If making up stories is not your thing, you can repeat classic ones you have read in your own words or tell stories about real people and events that have happened. Young children never tire of hearing about the special day they were born; older grandchildren are fascinated with stories about escapades their parents got into when they were young. Go ahead and embellish the telling – that's half the fun.

Take time for life skills play, including problem solving (e.g., puzzles, board games, and building toys), baking, sewing, gardening, building, fixing things around the house, cleaning, washing clothes and windows, writing letters and postcards, wrapping presents, etc. Kids love to help, so let them. Our reward is that proud look of accomplishment in their eyes, and knowing that we have helped them learn some important life skills.

A word here about gender differences. The grandparents we talked with said that boys are just as happy to cook and sew as girls are to build porches, do yardwork, and fix things. Liz told us that her granddaughter's favourite job is mowing the lawn and that with a little help from Grandma, her twelve-year-old grandson cut out, sewed, and decorated a Halloween costume from scratch, as part of a school project. It is also good for grandchildren to see their grandparents in non-gender-specific roles. Grandkids love to cook with their grandfather and to shovel snow or rake leaves with their grandmother.

You probably remember playing with cards, dominoes, puzzles, building toys, and board games with your grandparents. And while the memories of easy camaraderie may first come to mind, your grandparents were also helping you learn other important life skills such as fairness, problem solving, categorizing, mathematics, language, and co-operation.

Your grandchildren can also learn a lot and get to know you better by visiting you at work. Mark sometimes takes his grandchildren to visit Kristen, who is an emergency physician, during her lunch break. This gives them a chance to learn about health, emergency care, ambulances, and what it is like to work in a hospital. Stephanie, who is a writer, shares the book-making process with her grandchildren and encourages them to write stories on her computer and make "picture books" from a very early age.

Have fun with active physical play, including everything from crawling to climbing, wrestling, throwing, running, swimming, fishing, skiing, and other sporting activities. Bonnie told us how bathtub play has always been a favourite for her grandchildren.

> I always have a bag of simple things on hand – empty shampoo bottles and sieves, rubber ducks, floating fish, and bathtub hand puppets. Whenever my young grandsons get cranky or just before bed, I take them to play in the bathtub. I sit on the edge of the tub and take part in the imaginary scenarios when they invite me to. I never rush them and I wash their hair very carefully, so there are no tears. We finish up with a towel-off and lots of hugs, and cream on any little scratches or itches. Everybody feels good afterwards.

Preschoolers and young children love to go to the local park. Don't be shy about teaching them skills you have, whether it is how to throw a football, hit a golf ball, do a duck dive, or play hopscotch. Make sure that they are mature enough to learn a new skill so that they will experience success. As they get older, you can cycle, hike, or rollerblade together. Teenage children love to take you on in a game of tennis, especially when they start to beat you (and they will!).

Enjoy outings from time to time. Mary told us how her own kids complained when she "dragged" them to museums and out on nature hikes. Now they admit how much they secretly liked most of those outings and how much they learned along the way. It is easier with grandchildren. They are happy to be with you and less likely to pretend to be bored. Resist the urge to lecture, but feel free to discuss things you see together and to summarize important points. Choose outings that match the child's level of intellectual and physical development, as well as their likes and dislikes. A museum of natural history, a zoo, or an aquarium best fits a child who loves animals and bugs. Almost all children can find something of interest (or at least some buttons to push) in a science museum.

Experience nature together. Many grandboomers have a special affinity for nature and the environment. Over the years, you may have developed an interest in birds or wildflowers or trees or ocean mammals. You may like to row, sail, garden, or fish. You may love to pack a picnic and just go exploring. There is nothing more precious than sharing these interests with a grandchild, or enjoying the simple intimacy of walking hand-in-hand along a forest path. Granddaddy Ian told us his thoughts about this.

I'd like my grandson to look back and appreciate the times we had together exploring nature and doing things like fishing and camping. Last weekend we went for a picnic at the beach with our two-year-old grandson, Brett, and his parents. We had a great time exploring the tidal pools that are filled with baby crabs, seashells, and other interesting things. Brett was a little anxious about the seaweed until I explained that it was just grass underwater. He laughed and felt more comfortable touching it then.

Read with your grandchildren at all ages. New research confirms that reading aloud stimulates babies and that they learn words that are repeatedly read to them even before they can talk. Reading aloud, talking about stories and books, and encouraging your grandchildren to read on their own is one of the most important ways you can support their language and intellectual development. Books and magazines are a window to adventure and fun. Reading together gives you a chance to get physically close and to calm down. Be prepared to read a favourite story over and over, and *never* try to skip pages.

PLAY AND CHILD DEVELOPMENT
Through play children expand their understanding of themselves and others, their knowledge of the physical world, and their ability to communicate with peers and adults.

When children play they enter a state of "flow." This is when we humans are happiest, when we lose ourselves in what we are doing. Children who learn how to experience flow grow up to be happier adults.

The most important thing we can do is encourage play that is appropriate to our grandchild's stage of development, as well as his or her unique personality, and interests. While every child develops at his or her own pace, here are some guidelines on what to expect:

Infants use their bodies to explore the world around them. It is never too early to read and sing to babies, and to gently move their arms and feet about. Avoid overstimulating babies. Playing with babies in a caring, gentle manner helps them build trust.

Toddlers love their mobility and independence (look out!). Play that encourages this helps them learn autonomy. Toddlers start to see themselves as part of the family and develop skills to participate, especially language. Make-believe play helps them try out new roles.

Preschoolers develop skills for playing with others and experiment with how things fit together by playing with toys such as puzzles, water, and playdough. Their gross and fine motor skills develop rapidly, as well as their abilities with language. They learn how to plan ahead.

School-aged children learn co-operation and conflict resolution and how to follow rules when playing. They use new skills to organize and connect things (most love magic tricks and collecting specific objects). They develop special interests, skills, and hobbies, and need plenty of active play to release tensions.

Adolescents' play is closely tied to their friends and identity formation. They explore and take on leadership roles, as well as play that involves more risk (e.g., rock climbing). As they grow up and make their necessary break from their parents, many welcome the opportunity to still be kids with their grandparents, and to have a non-judgmental but wise playmate they can talk with.

QUESTIONS AND ANSWERS

Q: My grandchildren participate in organized sports. How can I best support them (and their parents) in these activities?

A: If you have the time, resources, and the inclination, you can support your adult children by taking your grandchildren to some games or practices. This is particularly helpful if there are several children in the family who need to be in different places at the same time. You can also help to pay for equipment or registration fees. But remember, it is the decision of the child and her parents whether or not she makes a commitment. Our job is to support these decisions and help our grandchildren have a positive experience. Even if you are not a hockey, basketball, or soccer fan yourself, it helps to get involved by

- having realistic expectations for your grandchild (not every child is or wants to be a star athlete);
- giving extra encouragement to girls, who typically participate in sports much less than boys;
- learning about the sport and supporting your grandchild's involvement;
- providing positive feedback and praise, based on effort and collaboration, not on winning;
- attending some games and enthusiastically talking about them afterward;
- helping your grandchild talk with you about their experiences with the coach and other team members;
- helping your grandchild handle disappointments and losing;
- modelling respectful spectator behaviour.

Q: Now that my grandkids are getting older, they want to do their own thing, like watch music videos and play computer games. They don't want their friends to see them playing with their grandparents! Does this mean that playful grandparenting stops when they get older?

A: As our grandchildren mature, their interests broaden and it may seem that they have little interest in playing or even being with us. This is normal. But your attendance at their dance performance or hitting balls at the driving range together will be remembered into adulthood. Invite them to share their world with you by asking about their music or including a friend on an outing to a movie. Follow their lead. If they initiate a hug in public, hug them back. With teens, you might choose to watch "their television show" with them, then ask them to play chess, cards, or trivia. Share jokes and encourage gentle teasing. Teens are looking for role models who are comfortable with themselves and can laugh easily.

Q: I am a long-distance grandparent who sees my grandkids only once a year. How can I be playful the rest of the time?

A: Selma Wasserman, author of *The Long-Distance Grandmother* (see Appendix), describes an idea she calls the "playful gift connection." Playful gifts are small and inexpensive and are more important for the connection they engender than they are as a toy in their own right. Playful gifts are sent frequently throughout the year and are always accompanied by a note, suggesting how your grandchild might use the object. They can range from a magnifying glass for a four-year-old child to instructions for a card trick for children aged eight and older.

Q: What about parties and celebrations? My grandmother used to organize a lot of these.

A: Playful grandparents understand the importance of ceremonies and celebrations for grandchildren. They do not have to be elaborate. The ritual of tea time with teapot, special cups, and sugar cubes can become a special time with grandchildren. Celebrating the first day of spring with a garden party or Easter with an egg hunt can become precious memories for children. Be sure to talk with the parents before you plan more elaborate parties, especially around birthdays and holidays. As children get older, ask them how they would like to celebrate their birthday. But be prepared! They may ask you to host a sleepover with six of their friends.

WHAT THE RESEARCH TELLS US

Pretending Is Not Just Child's Play

Studies show that when children pretend with parents and other adults, their play is more elaborate and extended than when they pretend by themselves. For example, a child playing alone might sit behind a toy steering-wheel, turning it and making engine noises. When an adult joins in they might also go on an imaginary trip. Later, the child will use this idea again in subsequent pretend games. One of the things that parents and grandparents communicate early on through pretend games is culture. Chinese grandparents, for example, more often use pretend situations than white Americans to teach social customs and routines, like how to greet a guest or teacher.

Source: University of Illinois, www.sciencedaily.com, Oct. 9, 1997.

Fit Kids Do Better Academically

The California Department of Education recently released results from a study comparing academic achievement and physical fitness. The results show that physically fit children do better academically, according to matched scores on the Stanford Achievement Test and the Fitnessgram, a state-mandated physical fitness test.

Source: California Department of Education, www.cde.ca.gov, 2002.

Grandparents Are Active Participants

According to the American Association of Retired Persons (AARP) Grandparenting Survey, 70 per cent of grandparents aged forty-five to sixty-nine had taken a grandchild to a local park or playground in the last month, over 50 per cent aged forty-five to seventy-nine had exercised or played sports with a grandchild. Over 50 per cent of older grandparents (aged sixty to eighty) had gone with a grandchild to a sporting event. Younger grandparents were less likely to have done so, perhaps because their grandchildren are too young

to attend, or because they are still employed and have less free time.
Source: American Association of Retired Persons (AARP). Grandparenting Survey, 2002.
www.aarp.org/confacts/grandparents

Benefits of Participating in Activities Outside of School

Children who participate in organized activities outside of school such as sports, music, the arts, or clubs tend to have higher self-esteem, interact better with friends, and perform somewhat better in school, according to recent data from the National Longitudinal Survey of Children and Youth (NLSCY). Young people aged twelve to fifteen, who rarely or never participated in organized sports, were more likely to report having lower self-esteem and difficulties with friends. They were also more likely to smoke.
Source: NLSCY as reported in *The Daily*, Statistics Canada, May 30, 2001.

THE LAST WORD

Here are some quotes from children we interviewed about playing with their grandparents:

> When grandparents read to us, they don't skip. They don't mind if we ask for the same story over again.

> Everybody should try to have grandparents, especially if you don't have television, because they are the only grown-ups who like to spend time with us.

> When Grampa takes us for walks, we slow down past things like pretty leaves and caterpillars.

> They show us and talk to us about the colour of the flowers and also why we shouldn't step on cracks.

They don't say, "Hurry up."

I like playing games with Grandma because neither of us knows the rules. It's more fun that way.

And then there was the exasperated grandmother, whose active grandson was always getting into mischief. Finally, she asked him, "How do you expect to get into Heaven?" The boy thought it over and said, "Well, I'll just run in and out, and in and out, and keep slamming the door until St. Peter says 'For Heaven's sake, Jimmy, come in or stay out!'"

Principle Seven

Be Consistent, Reliable, and Fair

Our role is to shape, not change the child, similar to how a gardener cares for a rose. To make that rose bloom beautifully, the gardener must tend to it, planting it in rich soil and feeding it regularly. But he can't change that flower's color, shape or scent.
– Drs. Bill and Martha Sears, pediatricians

Principle Seven: Be Consistent, Reliable, and Fair seems obvious to experienced grandparents. Both the parents and grandparents we interviewed ranked it as a high priority. Clearly, while children today may seem more independent and savvy, they need a steady, predictable environment just as much as their parents and we did as young people. But as you will see in this chapter, this principle is sometimes easier to talk about than to apply.

Grandparents have an opportunity to step back from the rat race (at least for part of the time) and to build a trusting relationship with our grandchildren that is solidly based on this principle. In doing so, we get a second chance to apply what we know is right. We support our children as parents by reinforcing their parenting decisions and by providing intergenerational stability in a rapidly changing world. Most importantly, we share the joy of seeing our grandchildren gain the trust, security, and confidence that are by-products of this principle.

THEN AND NOW

Peggy talks about her own experience with this principle as a child and as a parent.

> I had been raised in a family that valued the parent-child commitment and reliability above all else. My parents were always available, respectful, and interested in us. Fairness was an essential family ethic that was particularly important to my feminist mother and a father who coached young athletes. So as a parent, reliability and fairness came quite naturally to me. But I remember how hard it was to be consistent with my children. Sometimes, the kids wore me down. It was easier to capitulate than follow through.
>
> Then, my reliability was questioned when my marriage broke up and my husband and I divorced and became joint parents. Neither of us had left our children; we loved them even more. But in those days, parents who divorced were often seen as unreliable, and those that attempted the new-fangled arrangement called joint parenting were flying in the face of a tradition that said children need consistency and security in one home.

As we pondered what consistency, reliability, and fairness mean in the twenty-first century, we were struck by how it may be even harder these days to put this principle into practice. We wondered how grandparents can help when separation, divorce, and blended families have become more common. When young families are increasingly mobile and may move their home three or four times as their children grow up. When, unlike our grandparents who lived on the next street (or in our home), often we now live far away. When "fairness" has become much more complicated for children and young people who are bullied in school and led to believe by professional sport that winning at any cost is okay.

Grandparents need to be realistic about our ability to be on top of this principle all the time. But we welcome a second chance to apply it as a foundation for building a solid, loving connection with our grandchildren.

WHAT DO CONSISTENCY, RELIABILITY, AND FAIRNESS LOOK LIKE?

Some of the parents we spoke with expressed the wish that grandparents be more consistent in applying the rules that they had established for their children. Peter described his distress over how his parents allowed his young son to behave in ways that he was against.

> We have a "no hitting" policy at home that Mom and Dad know about but they still allowed our son to hit them when he was frustrated or wanted his own way. I was really upset about this until I realized we had never really sat down and discussed what they should do about it. We agreed that they would use the time-out technique and not condone hitting in any way. It didn't take long for Ryan to realize that the adults in his life would be consistent about hitting. It is just not allowed.

Some grandparents were frustrated with their children's insistence on consistent bed and meal times for their grandchildren. But when they talked it out with the parents, all agreed that consistency does not imply a total lack of flexibility, but rather that when changes are made, they are made for good reason. For example, while grandparents may try to maintain the same bedtimes their grandchildren have at home, it is not inconsistent to let the child go to bed a little later if you find they need more time to be comforted and soothed because they are sleeping in a different bed and room than normal.

Consistency applies to everyday practices such as the example above, and to the long-term. One of the advantages of having raised our own children to adulthood is our knowledge that growing up takes many years. We know that steady and predictable nurturing is important to children in the long run, and that we have a lot of time ahead.

In today's harried world, grandchildren need a recurring pattern of order and calm. They need to know that when they go to Gramma's house or when Grampa comes to visit there will always be time for hugs, talking, and just being. They need to feel that they can rely on us to be consistently positive, attentive, loving, gentle, and fun.

Remember how excited you were as a child when a grandparent or parent promised to take you somewhere special? Remember how disappointed you were if that promise fell through? Reliable grandparents only promise what they can deliver. That is why it is so important to decide your own vision and plan for how you will grandparent (see Principle One). Some grandparents want to and are able to be involved with their grandchildren on a daily or weekly basis. Others may choose to be less hands-on and act more as a mentor who supports special interests, passes on rituals, and is an active participant in family gatherings.

Reliable grandparents are there for their grandchildren and children, especially for important life transitions such as starting school and graduating, and in times of stress (see Principle Eight). They do not judge or preach. They listen well.

Gord, an uncle who plays a grandparenting role, told us how he made the effort to attend his niece's graduation from middle school in Halifax.

The summer before she started Grade Eight, I promised Valerie that I would come to her graduation. They make a big deal of this now, with a ceremony and a party and prom. Then I forgot all about it and left it too late to get a plane ticket at a reasonable cost. When I called to explain, I could hear the disappointment in her voice, although she said she understood. I hung up knowing that I just couldn't break my promise. So I took some time off work, packed up my computer, and took the express bus from Montreal. I arrived about three hours before the ceremony with flowers in hand.

Valerie ran into my arms and even invited me to the party afterward to meet her friends. I was so proud of her. And she was proud of me. I was the reliable uncle she had come to depend on.

Reliability becomes especially important when families break up. Bill, whose son James recently divorced, describes how he puts this into practice:

> During the breakup I made an extra effort to always be on time when picking up my grandchildren and never making a promise I couldn't keep. I wanted them to know that my commitment to them was unwavering. I told them over and over that I would always be a part of their lives, and I tried to show this in how I acted, too.

Fairness is not synonymous with treating each child the same or having the same expectations of each child. In fact, fairness is about accepting the uniqueness of each child and the varying needs of children and families at different times. Fairness can be a particular concern in step-grandparenting situations. Bill expressed a worry that we heard often when he explained that he was spending more time with his step-daughter and her two children than his own daughter, who was not yet married. The other grandfathers in the group reassured him that as long as he was open about this concern, his daughter would understand and look forward to the same kind of attention when she had children.

CONSISTENCY, FAIRNESS AND DISCIPLINE

Fortunately for grandparents, disciplining is really the parents' job, not ours. We are largely in the business of watching out for desirable behaviours that we can reward with hugs, verbal praise, and special activities. A certain amount of misbehaviour is normal. When conflicts and temporary moments of misbehaviour arise, savvy grandparents use listening, humour, distraction, or alternative choices instead of yelling, accusations, and lectures. We have learned that sometimes scooping up an overstimulated toddler and helping her into a calming bath is the best way to pull her out of a behaviour meltdown.

There is a great temptation for grandparents to give in to bad behaviour. It's easier, and besides we don't have to live with it every day. However, there will be times when you do need to discipline your grandchildren, especially if the behaviour threatens their safety or that of others, or runs counter to a fundamental value or rule that cannot be ignored. Setting up a few guidelines in advance and reacting in a consistent and fair way can help teach children about right and wrong, and help them find alternative ways to react when they feel angry, frustrated, or upset.

Mary told us how she uses deflection to keep her grandchildren at the dinner table. She believes that having this calm, consistent time together is important and that it is not unrealistic to ask them to stay until the meal is finished.

> The children know that they are expected to stay until the end of the meal and most of the time they are okay with this. But sometimes, the younger ones forget and they keep jumping up and finding reasons to leave the table. I used to hate it when my parents made me stay as a kind of punishment. So rather than come down on them about "the rules at our house," we deflect the issue by starting a game of "I Spy." The children get involved in the game. They stay at the table and even finish their food. There are no upsets and the kids learn that staying for family time can be fun.

WHAT GETS IN THE WAY OF CONSISTENT, RELIABLE, AND FAIR GRANDPARENTING?

Here are some of the common barriers that make this principle hard to apply and how some of the grandparents we interviewed have overcome these barriers:

I just don't know how to be fair about sharing my time with eight grand-children in three different families. I only have so much time and energy to go around.

Children and families have different needs at different times. Some live nearby, others a distance away. For these reasons (and others), it is impossible to give all of your grandchildren equal time and attention. Sometimes, this may mean giving more to those who need extra help. Sam, who has nine grandchildren living among several families, describes his philosophy of fairness and how he puts it into place.

> Being fair is not about strict rules deciding who gets what; it changes all of the time. I am constantly reflecting on where my children and grandchildren are at and who needs more time with us at a partic-ular time. I try to remain as even-handed as possible, but sometimes a particular child or family needs more help. I make sure I never leave someone out completely and I make special efforts to see the grandkids who live out of town. I try to use good judgement. My wife and I don't cave into the trap of taking five at once. Then nobody gets any personal attention.

I am unsure about how to discipline my grandchildren and which behav-iours are unacceptable.

It is important to talk with the parents ahead of time and to agree on what behaviour is acceptable and not, and how to respond to behaviours that are clearly problematic. These need to be defined in a concrete manner; for example, you may agree that swearing at someone is unacceptable, as is the purposeful destruction of prop-erty. Find out how the parents handle these situations and react in a consistent way if possible. For example, many parents use the "time-out" technique for dealing with situations like these. Susan describes how she used this technique with her three-year-old grand-daughter, Jennifer.

When Jennifer screamed and flung her dinner plate across the room, I picked her up immediately and took her into the next room. Jennifer and her sisters were surprised and startled. They had never seen their grandmother react like this before. I explained in a firm but calm voice that throwing a plate was dangerous (she could have hit her sisters), disrespectful, and unacceptable. I told Jennifer to stay sitting on the chair in the next room until she had calmed down and thought about what I had said. Then I returned to the dining room and explained to her wide-eyed sisters why Jennifer was having a "time out." Once she had calmed down (it took about five minutes), I asked her if she wanted to come back. Jennifer said yes, and quietly rejoined the family at the table. We talked about what else she could do the next time she didn't want her dinner.

My reaction was instant but I was glad my daughter-in-law and I had talked about the time-out technique beforehand. Afterwards, I knew that my actions were consistent with what her mother would have done.

Unlike our other children who have well-paying jobs, one of my daughters really struggles financially. I worry that our other children and their kids will resent the amount of financial support we give to her children.
Surveys show that grandboomers are more likely than previous generations to be able to help their grandchildren financially, often by paying for special interests such as music lessons, sporting activities, and trips. In some cases, financial support includes help with housing and other basic needs. Does fairness mean equal financial support for all grandchildren? Tom comments on how he deals with this tricky situation.

We have four children but give more financial support to one family because my daughter is a single parent and has very little money. I talk honestly with her siblings about this and they accept it. In fact, they try to help her, too. At the same time, I try to stay aware of how the other grandchildren are doing and to make sure that they are not losing out. If I start to have doubts about the balance, I talk openly about it with their parents.

How can I be fair when some of my grandchildren live six hundred miles away and others live in the same city?
Long-distance grandparenting is hard enough. Worrying that you are unfair because of distance only compounds the problem. Marnie believes that being a good long-distance grandmother can take just as much time and effort as grandparenting a child who lives three blocks away.

> Sure we have less physical time with our grandchildren who live at the other end of the country. But we sure spend a lot of time and effort communicating with them by e-mail, cards, letters, and phone. We also pay for them to come to visit and we make two trips a year to visit them. These extended times together help make up for not having weekly contact like we have with the grandchildren here. In fact, my granddaughter who lives in the city complained the other day that it was not fair because she didn't get to stay with us for ten days in a row.

I have three step-grandchildren as well as a granddaughter born to my daughter. Sometimes it is hard to be fair. I have a natural tendency to be closer to my birth-related grandchild. What can I do about this?
As modern families change and blend, grandboomers are more and more likely to find step-grandchildren becoming part of their extended families. Getting to know these children and making a real connection may be more difficult because you do not know their families of origin and likely were not around when they were very young. Nonetheless, they are your grandchildren. In fact, they may be more in need of a consistent, reliable figure in their life as a result of the divorce and remarriage of their parents. Here's what Ted says about how he handles this issue:

It's quite simple, really. I just think of my step-grandson as my grandson. I include him each time I make a decision about how to support and spend time with all of my grandchildren, whether or not they were born into my family. He knows I feel this way and we have developed a close relationship.

THE RELATIONSHIP BETWEEN PRINCIPLE SEVEN AND HEALTHY CHILD DEVELOPMENT

Being consistent, reliable, and fair relates to our growing understanding of an important aspect of child development called "temperament." Temperament is a set of inborn traits that are part of a child's distinct personality. They appear to be relatively stable from birth: some children are noisier than others, some are cuddlier, some have more regular sleep patterns.

When we understand how a child responds to certain situations, we can anticipate and prevent situations that might present difficulties for that child. We can also tailor our reactions to the particular temperamental characteristics of the child.

Classic child-development research conducted by doctors Chess and Thomas has identified nine basic temperamental traits that are shown in early infancy:

1. *Activity Level:* how active the child is generally
2. *Distractibility:* degree of concentration and paying attention when the child is not particularly interested
3. *Intensity:* how loud the child is
4. *Regularity:* the predictability of biological functions like appetite and sleep
5. *Sensory Threshold:* how sensitive the child is to physical stimuli (touch, taste, smell, sound, light)
6. *Approach/Withdrawal:* characteristic responses of a child to a new situation or to strangers

7. *Adaptability:* how easily the child adapts to transitions and changes like switching to a new activity
8. *Persistence:* stubbornness, inability to give up
9. *Mood:* tendency to react to the world primarily in a positive or negative way.

Obviously, it is easy to parent and grandparent children who have high levels of regularity, adaptability, approachability, and a positive mood. It may be harder to care for children who are highly active, distractible, intense, persistent, distant, or sensitive. Knowing that each child is born with a unique combination of these traits can help us build better connections with our grandchildren, and be more accepting of individual characteristics.

QUESTIONS AND ANSWERS

Q: My grandkids are always fighting about who gets to ride in the front seat or help me make dinner. How can I be fair and not cave in to the one that makes the most noise?

A: This is when it pays to develop a system for evenly distributing privileges such as riding in the front seat of the car, or who gets to go first in a board game. If you are with them for several days at a stretch, schedules are a great way to end squabbles over who gets to help cook, set and clear the table, or help with washing up.

Q: My grandkids are so hyper, their visits inevitably turn into bedlam as we race from one activity to the next. What can I do to create a more consistent and calm environment that doesn't leave both them and me exhausted?

A: Establishing consistent routines related to eating, sleeping, and quiet time can help bring order and calm to excited visits. Baking can be orderly when all ingredients are on hand, each child has an apron, and the routine begins with handwashing and ends with everyone helping to clean up. Grandparents can establish or continue consistent little traditions and everyday rituals such as holding hands and saying a grace before eating dinner, walking the dog together and stopping to chat with other dog walkers, or sharing a cup of hot chocolate and a chat before bed with older grandchildren. In the long run these everyday, predictable rituals are both calming and nourishing for all of us.

Q: Is it okay to talk openly about a child's particular strengths and even to compare them to others?

A: Describing a child's strengths helps build confidence and self-esteem. Comparing them with others should be handled carefully but can be especially effective when the child is better than you at something. For example: "It amazes me how you do that math at your age. I never did well in math when I was young and I still can't figure out the simplest algebra, let alone the stuff you are doing. I made up for it in history though. I was really good in that." In doing this, you are subtly getting some key messages across: you have strengths that I really admire; you can't be the best at everything; and we need to respect others for their unique strengths.

Q: Our parents are making life difficult for us because they are in constant competition with the other grandparents for time with our children and "winning" their love with gifts. What can we do about it?

A: This is an easy trap for grandparents to fall into, but one that ends up making things difficult for everyone, especially the parents. Hard as it may be, the best thing would be to sit down with all of the grandparents and tactfully tell them how their behaviour is stressful for you, and is sending the wrong message to your children. Tell them you know they are acting out of love. Encourage them to talk to each other and with you about how everyone can feel more comfortable.

WHAT THE RESEARCH TELLS US

Consistency Helps Kids Handle Stress

Megan Gunnar, Ph.D., from the University of Minnesota, has shown that by the end of the first year, children who have received consistent, reliable, warm, and responsive care produce less of the stress hormone cortisol. When they do become upset, they turn off their stress reaction more quickly. This suggests that they are better equipped to respond to life's challenges.

Source: Canadian Institute of Child Health. *The First Years Last Forever*, 2002.

Reliable, Caring Adults Help Children and Teens Overcome Adversity

Studies with adults who have overcome childhood and adolescent adversity such as abuse, neglect, and school failure show that a critical factor in their success was having at least one adult in their lives that consistently cared for them and advocated for them, especially in times of need. Psychologist Julius Segal calls these people "charismatic adults" who consistently display love and affection and make a child feel special. They do not need to be the child's parent and can be a grandparent, uncle, coach, or teacher.

Source: Brooks, R., and S. Goldstein. *Raising Resilient Children*. New York: Contemporary Books, 2001.

THE LAST WORD

Grandchildren Talk about Love

"When my grandma got arthritis, she couldn't bend over and paint her toenails any more. So my grandpa does it for her now all the time, even when his hands got arthritis too. That's love." – *Rebecca, age eight*

"Love is when Grandpa gives me most of his french fries without making me give him any of mine." – *Chrissy, age six*

"Grandma says love is what makes you smile when you're tired."– *Terri, age four*

"Love is when my Nanny makes coffee for my grampa and she takes a sip before giving it to him, to make sure the taste is okay." – *Danny, age seven*

"During my piano recital, I was on stage and I was scared. I looked at all the people watching me and saw my grandpa waving and smiling. He was the only one doing that. I wasn't scared any more." – *Cindy, age eight*

"Love is when Grandma sees Grampa smelly and sweaty and still says he is handsomer than Robert Redford." – *Chris, age seven*

"Grandma says you really shouldn't say "I LOVE YOU" unless you mean it. But if you mean it, you should say it a lot. People forget." – *Jessica, age eight*

Stay in Touch

Over the river and through the woods to Grandfather's house we go.

> – Lydia Marie Child,
> "Thanksgiving Day" in *Flowers for Children*

What do children value and need most from their grandparents? The same things that we treasured in our growing-up years: unconditional love and spending time together. Ideal grandparents are there for their grandchildren. They love their grandchildren because of who they are, not because of what they can do. They genuinely enjoy spending time with each grandchild. They are able to be "in the moment" and enjoy the magic of undisrupted connectedness. What a recipe for a love-in!

Many of the other chapters discuss how we can show our unconditional love – by being accepting, empathetic, fair, proactive, kind, playful, and open. This chapter deals with Principle Eight – staying in touch and being present (both physically and emotionally). Indeed, "being there" as a comforting presence for both adult children and grandchildren is one of the most important functions of grandparents.

For many grandboomers, this is easier said than done. The proverbial time crunch that most modern families face, and the phenomenon of long-distance grandparenting sometimes create problems that can seem insurmountable. Fortunately, there are many resources and practical ideas for dealing with these obstacles; you'll find recommendations for some great books and Web sites in the Appendix. Our purpose here is to reflect on why it is so important to stay in touch and spend quality time with your grandchild. The chapter provides you with some examples of how other grandparents are putting this principle into practice, and explores the potential of cyber-grandparenting, a modern idea for modern grandparents and their ever-so-clever grandchildren.

THEN AND NOW

Several of the people we interviewed reminisced about how as children they had spent time at Gramma and Grampa's house almost every day, helping in the garden, baking, exploring nature, visiting, hugging, and just chatting. After all, Papa and Nana lived just around the corner (or even in the same house). For most families, this is no longer a reality.

Most grown-up children leave their home community to pursue an education or a job. With easier access to inexpensive air travel and the globalization of many industries, young families are increasingly moving to other countries to work. At the same time, grandparents have become increasingly mobile themselves.

The following story, which was sent to us by a friend who drives a school bus part-time, reflects the casual way that many grandboomers use air transportation to make up for distance . . . and how their grandchildren perceive this.

> When I stopped the bus to pick up Chris for preschool, I noticed an older woman hugging him as he left the house. "Is that your grandmother?" I asked.
>
> "Yes," Chris said. "She's come to visit us for Christmas."
>
> "How nice," I said. "Where does she live?"
>
> "At the airport," Chris replied. "Whenever we want her, we just go out there and get her."

In North America, almost half of grandparents live at least two hundred miles away from their grandchildren. Even those that live in the same city are likely to face a forty-five-minute drive or a one-and-a-half-hour bus ride to their grandchildren's home in the suburbs.

The employment patterns of grandparents have also changed. When you think about your own grandparents, they were most likely retired. If your grandfather was still working, it was almost guaranteed that your grandmother was a full-time homemaker. Their own parents (your great-grandparents) were likely dead.

In the twenty-first century, this scenario is drastically different. Many grandboomers are helping to care for their own parents who are living well into their eighties, while trying to find time with their grandchildren and sometimes with children who have not yet left home. Most grandmothers in their forties and fifties are still working outside the home, and while most boomer men are retiring earlier than their own fathers, many go on to other part- or full-time work. Some grandmothers, who began their careers after the birth of their children, are at the prime of their working lives, putting in long, often stressful days at work.

Many boomer men and women do not have the luxury of retiring. In the Healthy Boomer Midlife Survey conducted by Peggy and her co-authors in 1999, financial and job insecurity was one of the key concerns of boomers in all walks of life. Gone are the days when most men worked for one company for thirty-five years and retired at age sixty-five with a gold watch and a secure, indexed pension. After years of job changes, downsizing, and layoffs due to economic recessions, paying off educational loans, and yes – an inability to save the way our parents did – most boomers are not financially prepared to retire. Many boomer women who worked at home or part-time in the labour force have little to no pension. Those who divorced in the sixties and early seventies generally were not awarded a portion of their husband's pension, and thus have many years to make up in contributions. In the United States, fears about financial security in retirement are exacerbated by high health-insurance costs and threats to the Medicare system that was designed to protect seniors when they became ill.

While many grandboomers are pressed for time due to employment and other family responsibilities, their children and grandchildren are also busy. Time is at a premium for families who are scheduled from six-thirty in the morning to ten o'clock at night, most days of the week.

ADDRESSING THE CHALLENGES OF STAYING IN TOUCH

Grandboomers talked to us about three major challenges to putting this principle into action: distance, finding enough time, and making it quality time.

The Distance Challenge

For many grandboomers, distance is the greatest barrier to being physically and emotionally available. Some make major life changes, such as changing their jobs or moving after retirement, just to be closer to their families.

When Bryn and Valerie retired, they settled down to living full-time at their idyllic country cottage in Northern Ontario. After two years of cold winters they wondered if they had made the right decision. When their daughter announced that a baby was due in January, they decided to rent a house in her neighbourhood in Ottawa, so they could be nearby for the birth and the first few months. Bryn describes the outcome.

> It worked out so well that Valerie and I decided to sell our country home and purchase a condo in Ottawa about five blocks from our new granddaughter's home. Our daughter and her husband are happy to have us nearby, especially because they have no other relatives in the city. We love the community and don't feel so isolated. But most of all, we love being close to our granddaughter. We have talked with her parents about what our role will be and everybody is excited about the move. Valerie says she has a much clearer picture about how we can help out, but still have our own lives to enjoy.

Other grandparents, who are unable to live nearby, make arrangements to be with their grandchildren as often as possible, while staying in touch on a regular basis by telephone, mail, and other means.

Lu and Tom, whose grandchildren are spread across Canada from sea to sea, make a point of staying in touch with all of their grandchildren by telephone and mail and with special visits whenever possible. But most importantly, they make it a priority to spend two weeks each summer at a family camp with their grandchildren.

> Going to Red Pine Camp each summer is a family tradition. Our grandkids can count on us being there and their parents can count on us to help them get there if they need it. Our two weeks together is intense and fun. We eat and sleep and swim and play together. We get to know each other intimately. The parents get a break and we get a chance to spend high-quality time with our grandchildren. We make beautiful memories. This helps make up for living far apart the rest of the year.

The Quantity of Time Challenge

Principle Nine: Be Organized but Flexible contains more information on overcoming the time-crunch challenge that many grandboomers face. Clearly, it helps to get organized and schedule well in advance. So does being flexible enough to take advantage of unexpected times you can spend with your grandchildren and their families. But the larger your family becomes, the harder it is to find the time.

Mary, who has eight grandchildren living in the same city, talks about her challenge.

> In addition to having eight grandchildren in the same city and a full-time job, I need to spend time with my mother, who has just moved into a retirement home. There aren't enough hours in the day. Needless to say, my schedule is pretty exhausting. I manage my life week-by-week, making sure that I see at least some of the

grandchildren and my mom each week. Sometimes I combine the visits. It is good for the grandkids to spend some time with their great-grandmother and she is energized by their company. Family parties are important. I make a point of connecting with each grandchild at these events, by taking them aside individually for a conversation, a big hug, and sometimes a walk. I have a tradition that when a grandchild reaches age ten we go on a trip together, just the two of us. This tends to cement our relationship and helps us remain close in the turbulent teen years ahead. Even so, I feel jealous of grandmothers that have retired and can spend more time with their grandchildren.

Mary has also described how she deals with another major challenge – the need to spend time with your grandchildren one-on-one. When you visit for a short time and/or you have numerous grandchildren, it may seem almost impossible to find time to be alone with each grandchild. But if you think back to your own childhood, it is likely that your best memories of time with a grandparent were when you were alone together. The research on child development bears this out. Quality relationships require time spent with children individually, when there is no competition for attention with siblings or other family members.

Fortunately, short periods of time seem long to a child. Grabbing little moments together and making a special individual connection at a family gathering may have to suffice. There may even be advantages to communicating long-distance. The nature of e-mail, letters, and the telephone is that the communication is with one child at a time. Use this opportunity to explore each grandchild's personal interests, hobbies, activities, and ideas. This is the information you need to build a one-on-one relationship that makes each grandchild feel special.

According to U.S. surveys, the average age of becoming a grandparent is now forty-eight. This means that most grandboomers will still be employed when their grandchildren come along. There is a tendency to say, "I'd like to be involved now but it will have to wait until I retire. Then I will devote all kinds of time to grandparenting."

Resist this way of thinking! Why? Because the literature on child development is clear. The first six years of life are an especially important window of opportunity. During this time the brain and personality are rapidly developing. Bonding and attachment to nurturing adults in infancy and the early years affect a child's happiness, health, and behaviour well into adulthood. The parents of course are the most important and influential people in a young child's life. Next important are the caregivers and relatives such as grandparents and aunts and uncles who spend time with young children.

Cheryl, a hospital maternity nurse, knows about the importance of the early years; she even teaches young parents about it. Then her daughter who lives in Australia, some five thousand miles away, announced that she was pregnant.

I knew immediately that I had to take some time off work, ideally for a month at a time, at least twice a year. It was a tough negotiation but I have seniority and there was another nurse who could fill in for me. With the blessing of my daughter and her husband, I was there for the birth and the first month of Jeffrey's life. My husband and I returned seven months later for one month. I do believe that Jeffrey and I bonded during those times. I got to know his rhythm and what his cries and gestures meant. He responded to me and to my voice. I fell in love again. Seven months after that, the family came home to visit and my daughter and her husband had their first time away from the baby. He is a happy, secure little boy, thanks to the nurturing and love he gets from his parents. But I also believe that we have helped.

My career has faltered as a result. I missed a promotion and had to accept a part-time designation, which means losing my full-time benefits. There is an attitude among some of the senior managers that I am not 100 per cent committed. It's ironic isn't it, that a workplace that should really understand why grandparents need some time away is still driven by old-fashioned beliefs that you can't do a good job when you take time off to support your family.

Not all grandparents are prepared to do what Cheryl did. If you are a working grandparent, you need to decide how you can comfortably make the time for both work and seeing your grandchildren. Maybe you will need to cut back on other commitments in your life, such as voluntary work or social engagements. But remember, those first six years are crucial both to your grandchild and your relationship. It is also the time when hard-working parents need the most help. Talk to your employer about this. It's high time that workplaces in North America gave increased support to the essential roles of parenting, grandparenting, and elder care!

The Quality of Time Challenge

In the Healthy Boomer Midlife Survey, the majority of respondents said that they wanted to be less busy, cranky, and fatigued, so that they would be better able to enjoy time with their families.

Fortunately, grandparents are not on duty twenty-four hours a day, seven days a week. We are less concerned about whether or not a child has done his homework and we have finished our housework. As Joan describes in the following story, there is something special about grandparenting that allows us to overcome the distractions of a busy life when we are with our grandchildren. The result is a truly beautiful experience.

When our son and daughter-in-law told us they were expecting their first child, they also asked if we would babysit the following summer for three weeks as they planned to attend a wedding in Italy. This seemed so far away and of course I said yes, looking forward to spending time alone with our first grandchild.

Derry was seven months old when he arrived to spend time with us at our cottage. It had been over thirty years since I had spent more than a day or two with a baby and I knew I had to be focused. We were in a quiet, beautiful environment, so I decided to look at this time as a retreat. I was reading a book (*Lost in Wonder* by Esther de Waal) and my next three weeks were indeed lost in wonder.

I took the time to become a part of Derry's world and feel that sense of awe in the midst of daily life. I attended only to him, I ate simply, I didn't entertain, and I slept when he slept. I was open to discovery through the eyes of a seven-month-old child. When we walked, I was not rushing or thinking about the future or dwelling in the past, I was in the present moment. We touched the bark on the giant white pine trees, we listened to the loons with our eyes wide open, we truly felt the water in the lake, and smelled the flowers and the herbs. It is unfortunate as adults that we lose that sense of wonder.

A baby takes nothing for granted and Derry took such pleasure in looking around his environment with "open" eyes. He never tired of patting the kitty, touching the leaves, being pulled in his wagon, and appreciating a smile, a kiss, or a hug.

Now that he is back home, I often take the time to stop and be in the moment and to be truly attentive. When our children were young I was always busy and I didn't "get it" about being in the present moment, but this is what makes grandparenting so special.

Being in the moment allows us to have quality time with our grandchildren. Quality times don't need to be long or expensive. It is the little things that mean the most – chats and hugs, sharing everyday chores, singing along to music in the car, and playing imaginary games together.

Nancy, who has a full-time job and a busy social life talks about how she makes sure that she spends quality time with her grandchild.

When Ellen comes over, I clear the decks. No sneaking in business calls. I take off my watch and give her my undivided attention. It isn't hard to do. The minute I crouch down to hug her, I feel a sense of happiness and relief. The urgency of my life seems to disappear. I try to share her world and she shares mine. Sure, I schedule things for us to do – she loves to help with household chores – but mostly we just go with the flow.

TIPS FOR LONG-DISTANCE GRANDPARENTING

Experts on long-distance grandparenting, such as Selma Wasserman who has published four editions of her popular book *The Long-Distance Grandmother*, believe that long-distance grandparents can be as effective as those that live down the street, as long as they are creative and persistent. She offers many suggestions on how to stay connected – from writing stories to communicating by phone and e-mail, to visiting and vacationing together. (See Appendix.)

Tony, a Canadian whose young grandchildren live in Israel, has begun to create personalized children's storybooks with photos on his computer as one way to stay in touch.

Being so far away from my grandchildren, especially in their early years, very often leads to pangs of loneliness and regret. My wife and I had discussed maybe reading them some children's books and sending tapes to them. Somehow we never got around to that, but it got us thinking about writing some very personalized stories for them.

I naturally had a lot of digital photos from their all-too-rare visits, so I thought I would try to write something using those images. That way, the three little girls would have something they could immediately relate to, and it would help them remember not only their grandparents (Zaidie Tony and Bubbie Marcy) but also the rather different scenery and way of life in Canada.

Starting with the images first made the storytelling quite easy. I found simple but profound joy as I wrote, reliving the wonderful memories of experiences we had with them and their parents. And there was more joy and fun when I was able to discuss the story with them over the telephone after they had read it, to hear their excited reactions first-hand, and answer their questions. They have asked for more, and I have promised them there will be.

CYBER-GRANDPARENTING

Most grandboomers are computer-literate to some extent, though not nearly as savvy as many of our grandkids. If you are a long-distance grandparent, getting on-line offers a whole new world of ways to connect with both your grandchildren and their parents. Even if you live in the same city, you may find e-mail or a chat network a great way to keep in touch.

As long as you and your grandchild each have a computer, you can use e-mail to communicate easily and inexpensively on a weekly or even daily basis, by sending short notes or simply sharing riddles and quizzes. You can download all kinds of information from the Internet and send graphics, cards, and articles about topics they are interested in. There are many Web sites that let you send cards for birthdays and other special occasions, often with animated cartoons and music.

These are the basics. Beyond this, the cyberworld offers some innovative and exciting ways to stay in touch. You may need to enlist the help of a local teenager to help you through a few complexities of the digital connections below:

- *Family Web pages:* There are many Web sites that will let you create a simple Web page. Once you have a Web page, it is relatively easy to load family photographs, and notes or jottings about special activities. If your grandchild has the page bookmarked on their Web browser, they will be able to see any new additions to the Web site you have created.
- *Digital cameras* have opened up the world of on-line photographs. Once you have a picture in digital format on your computer, you can attach it to an e-mail, mount it on a Web site, or include it in "storybooks" or collages. You can also print the

photos and put them in a photo album. Or you can mail them to your grandchildren. (They call this snail mail; it's old-fashioned but it still works.)

- *Scanners* allow you to scan photos or even drawings that your grandchild has done into your computer. Once the photo or drawing is in your computer you can e-mail it or post it on your Web site. So if you don't have a digital camera, a scanner will let you join the computer age. And you can even scan in old photographs, say of your grandparents, to create a Web site of the family's history.

- *Internet videoconferencing:* It is possible, using a high-speed Internet connection, to talk to your family on the other side of the world and see them at the same time. And what is really exciting is that the only cost is the equipment (and the Internet connection). There is no cost associated with the time you are talking and looking at each other. The cameras are inexpensive and sit on top of your computer. Recent advances in technology have improved the video quality and, while not perfect, it is now very acceptable.

- *Chatting on-line* is something your grandchildren will begin to do as soon as they can operate the computer. School-age children can spend hours having "conversations" by typing on their computer. One young teenager we know was asked whether she had ever had a fight with her boyfriend. "Only when chatting on-line, never in person," was her reply. You can easily join in and chat to your grandchildren by checking on your computer to see whether they are on-line or not.

- *Software* for creating family trees on your computer or family newsletters that you can e-mail to family members is widely available. The software has become much easier to use in recent years and will permit you to include photographs – even photographs of long-dead relatives that you scan into your computer.

- *Blogs* are journals that are posted on the Web. The name comes from "Web log" and has developed a cult following on the Web. While we can't imagine why anyone would want to post their private thoughts for everyone to see, there are grandparents who keep blogs – they are called bloggers. (Or are they grand-bloggers?) If you do start a blog, your grandchildren can read it any time they want to know what is going on in your life.
- *Gaming on-line:* There are now many games that are played on-line. The opponents in the game are on another computer, which could be thousands of miles away. Digital chess can be played on-line but most games are the shoot-'em-up variety in which the participants may stalk each other through a virtual landscape or a scene from science fiction. Some of the games are amazingly realistic and worth seeing. If you enjoy games you may want to try one with one of your grandchildren, or possibly several of them at the same time. Don't blame us if you get hooked!

Where do you start if you are a basic computer user and want to explore some of these options for staying in touch with your grandchildren? The Appendix provides you with more information, as well as numerous books and Web sites. And don't forget, if your grandchildren use your computer, be sure to install software that blocks access to pornographic and other inappropriate Web sites.

GRANDPARENTS AS HISTORIANS

Another aspect of staying in touch that is especially appropriate to the grandparenting role is providing your grandchildren and your adult children with links to their family's past.

Grandparents connect the generations together by passing on family stories and traditions. It is these stories and traditions that add so much meaning to our identities and our lives. Both of us have recently lost our fathers. This has reminded us of the importance of finding opportunities to share the wisdom, memories, and traditions that great-grandparents and grandparents bring to a family.

You can share stories about relatives, important events, family traditions, your own childhood, or the childhood of your grandchild's parents. This will help your grandchildren feel connected with you and other family members, in the past and in the future. In addition to telling stories there are other ways to encourage a sense of family history and tradition. Here are a few ideas:

- Carry on special holiday traditions, such as baking a special family treat or creating personal family gifts together that you made as a child. One grandmother, who always read a certain book to her children in the weeks leading up to Christmas, now reads the same book to her grandchildren.
- If you were born in another country, study the history, culture, and traditions of the country you came from with your grandchild. Take them to community festivals, museums, and restaurants that showcase your country of origin.
- If you grew up on a farm or by the sea and your grandkids live in a landlocked city, share your memories of what it was like. Consider taking them on a "farm" weekend or on an excursion to visit your hometown.
- Pass on the philosophies, parables, and sayings that you heard from your parents and explain what they mean. Some of Mary Jane's favourites that came from her Irish father include: "The thought is father to the deed" and "There is no virtue without temptation."
- If you are a long-distance grandparent, audiotape stories about how you and your ancestors grew up. Include some lively traditional music on the tape.
- Practice simple family rituals with your grandchildren that you learned as a child, such as holding hands to say grace before

dinner, or always sending a thank-you letter, or making a scare-crow each October, or letting family members choose the menu on their birthday.

• Pass on family mementos, letters, clippings, photos, heirlooms, and objects such as baby spoons and ornaments to your grand-children with a note explaining what they are, where they came from, and how they were used. When your parents die and you are faced with "cleaning out" their house or apartment, think carefully about what you can meaningfully pass on to their great-grandchildren.

Creating a family photo history can be a joint project with your adult children or a special project that they take on. Alicia explains how she and her siblings and in-laws created a living family history for her parent's sixtieth wedding anniversary.

We selected photos telling the history of Mom and Dad from the time they were young until now when they have eight grand-children. We had them made into a video with appropriate music, and into a PowerPoint presentation. After the anniversary party, each part of the family got a copy. Now each of us is adding our own family photos to the PowerPoint presentation so we have a living family history. My children never tire of seeing this special show about how they are connected to their grandparents and even relatives before them. They love the corny photos of me as a skinny kid with no front teeth, and photos of themselves as babies in Poppa or Nana's arms.

Don't forget to create historical remembrances of the lives of your grandchildren as they grow up. Miroslava describes how her mother, who lives in the Czech Republic, made special scrapbooks for her two Canadian grandchildren.

My mother kept every letter and drawing that my children sent her. She put these in a scrapbook, along with photographs over the years. These have become treasured possessions for both Luc and Karla.

Scrapbooks have come back into fashion. You will find lots of wonderful supplies at craft stores and can even take workshops on modern "scrapbooking."

BUILDING A LONG-DISTANCE RELATIONSHIP STAGE BY STAGE

Like all aspects of effective grandparenting, it helps to understand the various stages of child development so that you can use appropriate ways to stay in touch when you do not live close to your grandchild.

Infants: Early bonding is important so make every effort to visit your grandchild soon after birth. Babies make unbelievable leaps in development about every three to four months so if you want to be part of this, try to see them often. Meanwhile, ask the parents to send lots of photos. One young mom sent her mother both photos and e-mail notes about her daughter's progress throughout the first year. Grandma kept them in a file, to share with her granddaughter when she gets older.

Toddlers: Toddlers love the telephone and to hear your voice, even if they can't yet talk back to you. You can also send audio tapes with messages or you reading silly poems or singing. Don't worry if you can't carry a tune. Your grandchild will love it. Toddlers will also recognize your photo, so ask the parents to keep it on display in the child's room and even to have a nightly routine of saying "goodnight" to your photograph.

Preschoolers: All preschoolers are budding artists. Stay in touch with their creativity by asking the parents to fax or mail you some of their paintings and drawings. Take a photo of you standing proudly by them displayed in your kitchen and send it back with an appreciative note about how it enhances your decor.

School-aged children: These are the years to encourage your growing grandchild's interest in reading and the written word. Younger children especially enjoy stories written for and about them. Children of all ages love to get cards (on special and not-so-special occasions) that are addressed and mailed to them personally. Whenever you travel send postcards that have something of interest to your grandchild on the front, and then talk about it on the back. Find out what kinds of books they like and mail them one with a tape of you reading the story aloud. Children ages six to eleven quickly become computer-literate at school and most have access to a computer at home. If you are serious about keeping in touch, you need to get wired!

Preteens: Preteens become preoccupied with their friends so make sure you are ready to talk about their friends and what their "gang" is up to on the telephone – or even better – on real-time chat lines. Now is the time to give your grandchild a camera and prepaid film with a request to send you photos of their family, friends, and activities. When you get together, buy the materials and help them make a "memory" scrapbook about the visit. Graduation from public or middle school is a big and symbolic step. Try to be there. If you can't be there, send flowers, a special card, or a symbolic heirloom to mark this important passage and recognize that they are growing up.

Adolescents: Staying in touch with busy teenagers can be challenging, but once again small things mean a lot. Keep sending cards and notes marking special occasions in their lives. Be there for high-school graduation and other important academic or sporting events. Continue with rituals such as family birthday parties. Learn how to communicate on-line. If you share a special area of interest or expertise, offer to read and edit a school assignment or to work out a science experiment together on-line. Listen well and ask questions – about their friends, their music, and their hobbies. Consider hiring them to do odd jobs once a month that help you and enable them to earn some spending money. Plan a trip together to a place of mutual interest. If you want to ensure their participation, tell them they can bring a friend along.

QUESTIONS AND ANSWERS

Q: I am saving points and pennies so that I can visit my grandchildren who live in other cities. Are there some specific "rules of etiquette" about how often I should visit and how long I should stay?

A: These are all questions that you need to discuss with the parents ahead of time. Some families are more comfortable having visitors in their home than others. Most of the long-distance grandparents we talked to aimed to see their grandchildren two to four times a year (one grandfather called it "seasonal" visiting). They stayed from five to ten days, although those that travelled across the world went less often and stayed longer. A few grandparents slept in hotels or bed and breakfasts because their grandchild's home was too small to accommodate them overnight, but most stayed with the family. It is important to respect the family's rules, schedules, and need for privacy. Make it clear that you are here to offer help and support as needed, but especially to offer your unconditional love and time to your grandchildren and their parents.

Q: My daughter has asked my husband and me to be the primary care-givers of our grandson when she goes back to work in eight months. We adore our grandson and see him often. I am flattered and excited about the idea, but also a bit hesitant. Are we too old to be parents eight hours a day again? Will we resent giving up our independence and time off now that we have retired?

A: Approximately one-third of children are looked after by relatives while their parents work, including grandparents. Most grandparents who care for children report that they feel energized by the child and that they develop a deep and meaningful relationship. Other grandparents feel strongly that this is crossing the line from grandparenting to parenting (albeit, part-time), which they are not prepared to do. Ultimately, you must decide, taking into account the specific situation, wishes and needs of you, your grandson and his parents. Try developing a list of the pros and cons and discussing your feelings together. Sit down with the parents for an open and honest discussion. Then make your decision. Remember, it does not need to be forever. There may be alternatives to a forty-hour week of caregiving that suits everyone. Whatever you decide, the key is to ensure that you and your grandson continue to find the joy you have in your relationship.

Q: My wife and I have retired and are considering buying a condo in Florida to get away from the cold winter. We feel a bit guilty about leaving our children and grandchildren for six months a year. We have six grandkids – all under age eight. Should we wait?

A: This is a totally personal decision, which relates to your vision of how you want to grandparent and to your own health needs (see Principle One and Principle Ten). As we age, some people find that they remain far more physically and socially active in warmer climates where they can enjoy the outdoors. The good news is that long-distance grandparents can be (almost) as effective as those in the same town if they work at it. Presumably, there will also be opportunities for your children and their families to take a winter break and visit you. On the other hand, the years from one to six are the most important in terms of consistent face-to-face nurturing and helping out the parents with childcare. This is hard to do when you are not around on a day-to-day basis. Why not rent for a few years to see how it works out?

Q: The parents of my grandchildren will only allow me to babysit if I take them both at the same time. I want to spend some time alone with each of the grandchildren. They are very different in temperament and interests, and tend to squabble when they are together. I think part of the problem is that they almost never get time apart. What can I do?

A: Try telling the parents about your desire to have the children separately so that you can build a special relationship with each child. Initially this could be for short periods of time, such as an afternoon shopping trip or a nature walk. Reassure both the parents and the other grandchild that his or her special time with you is coming up next . . . and be sure to follow through. It's probably best to ignore sibling rivalry as a reason for babysitting them separately. Concentrate on the positive instead – how important it is for you to be able to give your energy, time, and love one-on-one, at least some of the time.

WHAT THE RESEARCH TELLS US

Grandparents Stay in Touch

About one-third of Canadians sees one of their grandparents once a month or more. Forty-one per cent see a grandparent less than once a month, and 20 per cent haven't seen their grandparents in twelve months. Many grandparents keep in touch by phone or letter: 13 per cent on a weekly basis and 22 per cent monthly.

Source: Health Canada. *Seniors Info Exchange,* based on Statistics Canada data, 1998.

According to a recent survey by the American Association of Retired Persons (AARP), over three-quarters of grandboomers saw their grandchildren between once a week and once a month, despite the fact that the majority (68 per cent) are employed. Principal barriers to more frequent contact are living too far away and their grandchildren's busy schedule.

Source: American Association of Retired Persons (AARP). Grandparenting Survey, 2002. www.aarp.org/confacts/grandparents

THE LAST WORD

The following was written by Karla, a Canadian university student whose parents came from the Czech Republic:

What I remember most about having grandparents in another country was being able to visit a completely foreign country but at the same time, feeling a great deal of comfort and security because it was my family that I was staying with. Going to visit a foreign country as a tourist is a completely different experience. When you are visiting family, you don't feel so estranged from the country and immediately you have a special relationship with it.

Sometimes, it felt a bit overwhelming. I remember arriving at my grandparents' home when I was younger and having these two people I barely knew being absolutely ecstatic to see me. But it is that enthusiasm that I began to love over time. When you only rarely get to see your grandparents, it makes the times you do see them that much more exciting. Having grandparents in another country creates a whole new dynamic within the family. It makes you appreciate them much more because you see them so little and when you do, you always want to make the most of your time together.

If I had children and their grandparents lived in another country, my main concern would be ensuring that they were able to foster some sort of relationship. Perhaps one of the best ways to do this is to teach them the language, so that communication is possible. Knowing the language also allows children to have a connection with their grandparents that they do not have with almost anyone else. Frequent visits and quality time spent together would be my main concerns in terms of encouraging my children and their grandparents to have a healthy relationship.

Be Organized but Flexible

He flung himself from the room, he flung himself upon his horse,
and rode madly off in all directions.

— Stephen Leacock

Boomers are too busy to leave grandparenting totally to happen-stance if we want good relationships with our grandchildren and their parents. Principle Nine: Be Organized but Flexible is intended to make life easier for grandparents, parents, and grandchildren alike. With a little planning, our homes, our visits, and our special times with our grandchildren can be more relaxing and rewarding for everyone. At the same time, we need to be flexible. Life in the twenty-first century is too fast-paced for us to be rigid. Call it the "ying" and the "yang" of modern grandparenting logistics: be organized but also willing to change your plans at the drop of a hat.

In Principle One, we looked at the bigger picture in terms of deciding what kind of grandparent you want to be. In this chapter, we take it a step further by addressing planning for your everyday life as a grandparent. The tips and suggestions are mostly "lessons learned from the front" and come from the experience of the authors and other grandparents.

THEN AND NOW

Time has become a luxury. Even grandchildren seem busier, often occupied with school or after-school activities most evenings and weekends. For busy boomers, scheduling time for grandchildren can be a challenge, especially for grandparents with numerous grandchildren from various families. When step-grandchildren and competing grandparents enter the picture, you now have a logistical nightmare. In the past, most grandparents didn't feel this time crunch, especially grandmothers who seldom worked outside the home. Today, few boomers have the luxury of being totally spontaneous grandparents.

There are more safety standards for children than when we were parents. Car seats have to meet specific criteria and are sometimes difficult to install properly. Cribs, playpens, high chairs, strollers, and many toys from our day are now known to be unsafe. We can't just haul our old child gear up from the basement when the grandchildren come to visit. If we want them to spend time in our homes, we need to be prepared.

Modern parents themselves are more organized, especially when both work outside the home. Grandparents should not be surprised when their adult children hand them a four-page list as they drop off their grandchild for the first time. Rather than take the list as an indication that we have forgotten everything we knew about raising children, we should simply appreciate the time and energy our adult children have taken to make our lives a little easier and their children safer.

WHAT GETS IN THE WAY OF BEING ORGANIZED AND FLEXIBLE?

Seasoned, busy grandparents understand the need to be organized yet flexible, especially those with more than one grandchild. Regardless, planning ahead does not come easily for everyone. Grandboomers discussed some of the pitfalls and how they handle them.

Just Not Enough Time in the Day

Being too busy is not an issue for working grandparents only. Retired grandboomers are leading full, interesting lives, often travelling for a portion of the year. With few exceptions, gone are the days when the family had regular Sunday night dinners at Grandma and Granddad's.

When grandchildren are young, it is easier to fit them into your schedule. As they get older, it gets more complicated because of their after-school and family activities. Grandboomers have to be more resourceful if they want to have regular contact with their busy grandchildren. One grandfather drives his granddaughter to and from gymnastics each week. It gives them time alone in the car and an opportunity to go for an ice cream sometimes on the way home. Another gave art lessons to his grandson for his birthday and signed himself up at the same time.

Grandparents with more than one grandchild have the added challenge of trying to be fair when organizing time with grandchildren (see Principle Seven). Kari and Eric have five grandsons. Having them over together can be chaotic with little opportunity for quality time, so they set up a schedule where two grandchildren sleep over every Friday night. Grandparents like Myrna and Norm, who have grandchildren scattered across the country, make sure they schedule regular visits with each family alone, and bring the whole family together at least once a year so all the cousins can get to know one another. These annual family holidays are planned far in advance and subsidized by the grandparents.

Being organized as grandparents also includes setting up our homes so they are safe and comfortable for grandchildren. One single grandmother recalled scrambling late one evening to borrow a crib for her new grandson after being informed by the distressed parents that her ten-year-old crib was not safe. Actually, the word used to describe the crib was a little stronger: "death trap."

Luckily I have a younger friend nearby whose children had recently outgrown their playpen. It was perfect for Kristen. I eventually bought it along with a high chair, bumper seat, and stroller. I'm now more organized. My house is totally equipped for Kristen and all I have to worry about is how often I get to see her.

Many busy grandparents have learned to be more efficient *because* they are so busy. They buy presents and cards for their grandchildren well in advance, knowing that they may be pressed for time when the occasion arises. They stock their home with books, toys, and craft supplies. One couple have a sleepover kit ready for each grandchild that includes pyjamas, fresh undies, a T-shirt, and toothbrush. And then there is our friend Peggy R., who went the whole nine yards and converted a bedroom into a baby nursery for her first-born grandchild.

Sometimes It Is Hard to Be Flexible

It can be frustrating if parents make a habit of calling at the last minute to ask busy grandparents to babysit, or even worse, coming over unannounced and expecting them to mind the grandchildren. Rather than get resentful, grandparents need to have an open conversation with the parents and clarify the expectations on both sides.

For grandparents who have to share their grandchildren with numerous other grandparents because of separation or divorce, being flexible when planning for special times like Christmas, Thanksgiving, birthdays, graduations, and weddings is also difficult but important. Modern parents are under enough stress without us grandboomers adding to this. Mary Jane and her husband, Michael, talk about how they handle Christmas.

We have a blended family of four grown children, three of whom have children of their own. We'd love to see them all on Christmas Day but they have many grandparents to see, plus they need some time alone as a family. At first, we tried to organize a time when we could be all together on Christmas Day. We soon decided that the most important thing for them and for us was just being together as a family. The day didn't matter. Now Michael and I spend Christmas Day with our siblings and we schedule our family time over the next few days. Occasionally I feel wistful on Christmas morning because it is such an emotional time, but I have to say it is better for everyone concerned. We have the whole day together and everyone is more relaxed.

We Need to Be Spontaneous

Many grandparents guard their free time fiercely. They may be working with little time to spare or recently retired and savouring their new-found freedom, or perhaps the memory of raising their own children is still too vivid. For all of these reasons, some grandboomers are reluctant to commit to specific times with their grandchildren. While this is totally understandable, the young parents we spoke with were upset by this inability to make a commitment. One young couple expressed it this way:

> We just can't rely on my parents. They always want to keep their options open until the last minute. We can't wait until the zero hour to know if they are going to babysit or even come over for a visit. We're not sure what this is about. It's not like they don't understand; after all, they raised five kids.

Perhaps these grandparents are just tired! Nevertheless, by refusing to plan ahead, they make it difficult for their children to plan as well. These young parents have just recently decided that they will ask them to babysit only in an emergency.

For grandboomers who overcome the hurdles, the rewards for being organized are worth the effort: less stress, more quality time with their grandchildren, and happier parents. We recognize, however, that some grandparents are faced with serious obstacles in their lives, and getting organized is the least of their worries.

Many of the tips and suggestions that follow are plain common sense. The ones that deal with safety issues are non-negotiable. Parents today have better information about the potential risks for children. Boomers can no longer rely solely on the safety standards we adhered to when our children were younger.

SOME SUGGESTIONS FOR BEING MORE ORGANIZED

Dr. Arthur Kornhaber, the guru of grandparenting, feels that a grandparent's house should be a second home for grandchildren – a retreat where they can explore and discover family artifacts and come across the unexpected. This is the place where holidays are celebrated with the whole family. He says that we should create a special space that is theirs, where they can do no wrong. A tall order and certainly not every grandparent's cup of tea.

Even if we are not hoping to create a second home for our grandchildren, there are things grandparents can do to make our homes safer, our time with our grandchildren more rewarding and our lives less stressful. The tips and suggestions that follow are organized into the following categories:

- Organizing your home
- Organizing for safety
- Planning for visits
- Planning for babysitting
- Planning for financial support

Organizing Your Home

Newborns: At this stage, we don't need much in the way of baby gear. Newborns don't roll over so they can sleep on a bed or a couch. While most mothers carry essential baby supplies with them, there are a few things we can keep on hand for newborns: diapers, baby wipes, rash creams, and receiving blankets for spitting and changing babies. Today's parents have many choices in baby products and are often attached to specific ones, so be sure to check with them for preferences.

Infants: Once babies are about three months, you need to provide them with a place to sleep. Many grandparents have found that one of the best options is a playpen. The modern playpens are portable, light, and store easily. Just be sure that any playpen or crib you buy meets the current safety standards.

The potential list of things you can buy for your home at this stage is endless. It depends on how keen you are to have your grandchildren over, how often and for how long, and your particular living conditions. Some grandparents are unable or unwilling to invest in baby paraphernalia. It is certainly not necessary, nor does it mean that they are not good grandparents; nonetheless, most grandparents have found that it encourages their children to bring the grandchildren over more often because it makes life easier for them.

If you decide to make this investment, talk to the parents and make sure you are respecting their standards for safety. One of the best places to acquire most baby gear, especially second-hand equipment, is at garage sales. In our experience, the problem for boomers is not the cost of baby gear, but finding storage space, especially for those who have downsized their homes. Plastic storage bins that fit under the beds come in handy for "space-challenged" boomers.

The items below are useful to have on hand for grandchildren up to age two, when they are visiting with their parents or you are babysitting them in your home.

- high chair/bumper seat
- stroller (look for big wheels for easy manoeuvrability)
- car seat (check safety standards)
- baby bottle, baby drinking cup, non-breakable baby dishes, baby

spoons (including the ones that change colour to indicate excessive heat)
- diapers, rash creams, baby wipes
- soother (same brand as parents use)
- receiving blankets and colourful floor blanket
- age-appropriate books (soft ones for babies)
- age-appropriate toys, including bathtub toys, as this is usually a favourite activity for babies and grandparents alike
- thermometer for babies since "what is her temperature?" is often the first question you will be asked if you need to consult a medical professional.

Some grandparents who see their grandchildren frequently, keep on hand an extra sleeper and a supply of baby food that they can use if required. Be aware that some foods are no longer considered safe for babies and toddlers (see Principle Three).

Toddlers: Grandchildren ages two to three require little in the way of additional children's furniture. Many of them begin sleeping in beds around this age so you may want to buy a safety bar that can be attached to the side of a bed or a couch. Toddlers usually sit in a bumper seat for meals although many insist on sitting on a regular chair like grown-ups, with the aid of cushions or telephone books. Things you may want to buy for your home at this stage include:

- appropriate diapers if not yet toilet-trained
- an extra pair of undies (when toilet-trained), pyjamas, and a sweater, sweatshirt, or light jacket
- a special blanket that they use when sleeping over
- a special stuffed animal that might replace "Pooh Bear" in case Mommy and Daddy forget to pack him
- toothbrush and children's toothpaste

- emergency kit containing Band-Aids (toddlers love Band-Aids) and basic first-aid cream
- night lights for their bedroom and the bathroom
- their own plates, cups, bowls, and spoons
- toys (see Principle Six for more ideas on types of toys and the Appendix for Web sites concerning toys and safety)
- age-appropriate books (toddlers never get bored reading their favourite books, so you don't need many)
- outdoor equipment such as a sandbox, balls, bats, swings, wading pool, and hose
- portable phone because you never want to leave a toddler alone while you answer a call.

Savvy grandparents keep toys and books in a special place that is accessible to the toddler. For example, Pat and George have a room off the kitchen where they store their granddaughter's books on a bottom shelf.

> Abby has as many books at our house as she does at home, most of them bought at garage sales. When Sarah announced that she was pregnant, I asked them one thing: that they would read to the kids. Education is important to us. When we can't find Abby, we know she is reading her books. She pulls people into her little room and says "sit, read." She loves her books.

Grandchildren love to have a place that they can call their own. It could be the bottom shelf of a bookcase, a drawer with their crayons and books, or a basement room that contains their "things." Rediscovering these familiar objects becomes part of the magic each time they go to Grandma and Granddad's.

Preschoolers: Three- and four-year-olds love to play with and "help out" Grandma and Granddad. Here are a few items that you might consider acquiring at this stage:

- a special apron for each grandchild to wear when baking or doing crafts
- balls and water toys
- craft supplies
- dress-up clothes, including old hats, jewellery, and scarves.

School-aged children: From age five on, the things you buy for your home will largely be driven by the activities you will be doing with your grandchildren. Peggy found that her best investment for her six grandsons has been a plastic hockey net and hockey sticks. Mary Jane found that both her granddaughters and grandsons love the play kitchen that she set up in the basement playroom – furnished mostly through garage sales.

Organizing for Safety

Safety is the most important consideration when organizing our homes for grandchildren. It's been a while since most boomers worried about leaving a pair of sharp scissors on the coffee table. As a result, there are potential safety risks for little ones in many areas of our homes. Experts in injury prevention insist that there are no such things as "accidents." Virtually all injuries can be prevented with a little forethought, consistent supervision, and the use of good judgement. The following list, while not comprehensive, suggests some of the key areas to consider when childproofing your home. The Appendix lists Web sites and books where you can find additional information.

When small children are visiting

- Install safety gates at the top of all stairs. Infant-walkers are now banned in Canada, largely because of the number of accidents involving unblocked stairs.
- Place safety covers on electrical outlets that young children can reach.

- Latch any kitchen cupboards that contain harmful objects such as sharp knives, matches, or plastic bags – or remove these objects.
- Check to make sure that your houseplants are not poisonous.
- Remember bathroom safety: water temperature, not leaving children alone, keeping the toilet lid down – Grandpa.
- Don't drink hot coffee or tea when holding your grandchildren.
- Think twice about using tablecloths with young toddlers around. They can pull the cloth and whatever is on the table onto themselves.

Precautions for all children

- Keep medications, cleaning supplies, and other hazardous materials in their original containers and out of reach, including in the garage and basement.
- Make sure you can open your bathroom door from the outside; children have been known to lock themselves in.
- Keep emergency phone numbers handy, including the poison-control centre and a nurse's hotline.
- Keep a basic first-aid kit handy, which includes a thermometer, bandages, and antibacterial cream.
- Be careful when microwaving children's food because it gets very hot on the inside. Always stir and test it yourself before serving.
- Check your hot-water tank to make sure it isn't set too high: children of all ages can easily be burnt by tap water that is set too hot.
- When buying toys for your home, think of safety. If in doubt, check with safety standards posted by governments.

Areas requiring constant supervision

- Be careful of open windows and screens.
- Teach children to stay away from any hot surfaces such as stoves and fireplaces.
- Sharp corners on furniture are dangerous, especially when youngsters run around chasing each other (or Granddad). Rubber bumpers are available for coffee-table corners.
- Be vigilant when children are around water and follow all swimming pool safety regulations. Even a large bucket of water or a small pond can be dangerous for youngsters.
- If you have a pet, don't make assumptions about how it will react to grandchildren. Err on the side of caution.
- Injuries to children can occur in both low-speed and high-speed car accidents. There are specific directions for installing infant car seats. In many communities, personnel at the local fire-station will ensure the car seat meets the safety standards and show you how to install it correctly.

Planning for Visits

When the grandchildren and their parents are visiting in your home, be prepared to relax your housekeeping standards. You will probably find the house littered with shoes, clothes, toys, suitcases, and depending on the age of the grandchildren, baby gear. Make sure the house is childproofed before your grandchildren arrive.

Be prepared to feel pooped at the end of the visit – grandchildren are fun but tiring. If possible, try to spend one-on-one time with each grandchild during visits, either by going for a walk, reading a book, or running an errand together.

Plan simple meals. Accept help from your adult children and their partners if they offer to bring food. The less time you spend looking after everyone else, the more you will be able to enjoy your grandchildren.

Don't schedule anything for the first few hours after they leave. You might need a nap. Or, as one grandfather put it, "After the grandchildren leave, I always take to my bed."

Planning for Babysitting

Minding grandchildren in your home may seem like no big deal at first. Guess again. Depending on the ages of your grandchildren and the number you are minding there are many things to think about in advance. The first suggestion is to clear your plate because grandchildren can take a lot of time and energy. Let people know you are babysitting. Give some thought to how you might spend your time with the grandchildren, remembering that you don't have to entertain them every waking hour.

Make sure you are aware of any allergies or recent changes in your grandchild's life such as school issues, discipline problems, or progress in toilet training. Double-check that the parents have brought any necessary medications with the instructions. Confirm that they have packed sleep aids such as "blankie" or Pooh Bear, and have included the right clothing – or you may find yourself shopping for bathing suits or sweatshirts. Of course, this may be a welcome excuse for some grandparents!

Oh, don't forget, plan to have fun.

Planning for Financial Support

As a group, we boomers are better off than previous generations and the ones that follow us. Some of us will benefit from our parents' frugality and inherit money. We have had more work opportunities and more job security than our kids. Hopefully, we have managed to put some money aside for retirement.

Boomers have often been accused of being self-centred and have even been nicknamed "the me generation." But when it comes to grandparenting, studies show that boomers are just as generous or more generous than previous generations. Many grandboomers pay for "extras" for their grandchildren that parents can't afford, such as music lessons or sporting activities. Others provide financial help with basic necessities such as daycare and housing. In the U.S., many grandparents help with medical and dental costs because these are not covered by public insurance. Some grandboomers set aside money and investments to help with their grandchildren's education.

Sharing our wealth while we are alive benefits everyone. Our adult children need financial help most when they are raising our grandchildren, and we get the joy that comes from seeing that we have made a difference. Not every boomer is in a position to spend extra money on their grandchildren. Some are saving for their own retirement. Others are struggling just to make ends meet, especially grandmothers who live alone. For those who can afford to help out, here are some basic questions to ask yourself.

- What is most important to you and what would be most helpful to a particular grandchild? For example, one grandmother who values education highly, recognizes that her youngest grandson will not go to college or university, while his older sister most likely will, and offers financial assistance accordingly.
- If you are paying for extra activities, what do you do if the parents want one activity and you think another is more beneficial for your grandchildren? Do you give the money to the parents or pay for the activity yourself? One grandfather was concerned the parents would spend the money on cigarettes, so he paid for his grandson's soccer directly.
- How willing are you to help with necessities such as groceries or paying off debts? What will you expect in return?
- Will you contribute to your grandchildren's educations? If yes, how will you do this? An education or trust fund? Annual cheques to be deposited in a grandchild's bank account? What

happens if you find out the parents haven't opened an account and have spent the money on other things?

• What is the role of the other grandparents? If you are separated or divorced, will you talk to your ex-partner about working together to provide financial support?

• Will you give your grandchildren part of their inheritance now?

We cannot provide the answers to these questions. We do suggest that grandparents and parents discuss together how to fund grandchildren's activities and education. In addition, every grandparent should talk to a financial adviser about providing for their grandchildren.

SAFETY AND CHILD DEVELOPMENT

Unintentional injuries are the number-one cause of death and the second most common cause of hospital visits for children and adolescents in Canada and the United States. Overall, motor-vehicle injuries are the leading cause of death, and falls are the leading cause of hospitalization due to injury, among children and youth from ages one to nineteen.

Several factors influence the type and number of injuries among children, including gender, socio-economic status, and the child's developmental level. Boys are more likely to be injured than girls, and being poor is associated not only with higher rates of injuries, but also with more severe and often fatal injuries. Another important factor is the child's stage of development, as outlined below. Attentive grandparents need to be aware of the risks at various ages and to actively take steps to prevent injuries when their grandchildren are in their care. Knowledge, supervision, and good judgement are the keys to preventing injuries.

Infants: The most common cause of hospital visits is falls from heights (for example from changing tables or beds). Other causes of injuries or death include suffocation (largely caused by entrapment in cribs made before current safety standards went into effect), choking, burns from water or food, drownings in bathtubs, and motor-vehicle incidents. The latter arise from not riding in a safety seat, riding in an improperly fitting or incorrectly facing car seat, or riding in a car seat that is not properly secured.

Toddlers: While injuries related to motor vehicles remain a major concern, injuries at this stage are often due to the toddler's increasing curiosity and mobility. These include falls down stairs or from furniture they have climbed on, poisonings from open medicines and home cleaners, choking on small objects such as buttons or coins, drownings in large buckets and planters, cuts from sharp objects such as knives or tools, burns from playing with lighters, and suffocation from playing with plastic bags or blind cords.

Preschoolers and early school-aged children (ages 4 to 9): Children this age are at increased risk for motor-vehicle pedestrian injuries related to crossing intersections, running into the street, and colliding with cars while on tricycles and bicycles. Falls from bicycles and playground equipment can result in cuts, broken bones, and head trauma, especially if the child is not wearing a bicycle helmet. Strict supervision is required around swimming pools, rivers, and ponds.

Preteens (ages 10 to 14): Severe injuries related to motor vehicles, including four-wheelers and snowmobiles, are high among this age group and falls are again the number-one cause of hospitalization. Sports injuries become more common, as are burns, broken bones, and cuts related to active outdoor pursuits.

Adolescents (ages 15 to 19): In this age group the main causes of injury relate to motor-vehicle incidents and suicide attempts. While grandparents may have little direct influence on these factors, they can play an important role by engaging teen grandchildren in confidential discussions about driving habits, drinking and driving, depression, and the warning signs of suicide.

QUESTIONS AND ANSWERS

Q: We plan to take my two grandsons (aged seven and nine) on a two-week car trip to Prince Edward Island this summer. We'll stay in a cottage by the ocean when we get there. How can we make the long drive fun – and keep our sanity?

A: In *The Long-Distance Grandmother*, Selma Wasserman offers some excellent advice for happy times on the road with grandchildren. First, check with their parents that they are ready to be away from home for an extended period of time. Be sure that you are also ready; if you are having second thoughts about your energy or stamina, postpone the idea until you feel better. If it is a go, involve the children as much as possible in the planning. Prepare them well for what you expect, especially regarding safety issues. Have "en route" activities for them to do; plan to stop early and choose accommodations with swimming pools and other child-friendly facilities. Call home frequently so they can describe their adventures and record the journey in a memory scrapbook with lots of photos, pamphlets, and captions. The Web sites in the Appendix will also lead you to more tips for travelling with grandchildren.

Q: Am I the only grandparent who can't figure out how to operate the modern car seats, high chairs, playpens, and strollers?

A: No, you aren't alone. Baby gear today is safe but complicated. We need clear instructions on how to install a car seat, remove the tray in a high chair, collapse and open a playpen, and lower and raise the bar on a crib. The list goes on. One grandmother recalls her first experience with a modern stroller. She was so excited about taking Finn for the day that she didn't pay much attention to her son as he gave instructions on how to open the collapsible stroller. Imagine her frustration and embarrassment when she couldn't open the stroller once she had reached her destination. She had to drive back to her son's home and get a lesson.

Q: Now that our children are gone, we have finally furnished our home in a style that we love. Should we remove all the breakables and cover our new couch or can we teach our grandchildren to respect our home and leave it as is? Their parents are pretty relaxed in their home.

A: That is your choice. It depends on the age of your grandchildren and how much effort you are prepared to spend teaching them to respect other people's property. If you do leave things around, be prepared for the occasional mishap and make sure you have a good stain remover. Valuable, fragile articles should always be removed. If your grandchildren visit infrequently, your time might be better spent enjoying them, rather than keeping guard over your knick-knacks and furnishings. In addition, your adult children will feel a lot more at ease, knowing that your valuables are safely out of reach.

WHAT THE RESEARCH TELLS US

Put Your Medicines Away
A study by the U.S. Consumer Product Safety Commission showed that over one-third of unintended childhood prescription drug ingestions involve a grandparent's medication. Grandparents often have non-child-resistant prescription vials or loose pills out on tables, kitchen counters, or in purses or pockets. Children swallow these medications when they are visiting grandparents or when the grandparents visit them.

Source: U.S. Consumer Product Safety Commission, www.cpsc.gov

Grandparents Don't Always Play It Safe

According to a survey carried out by Nissan, 21 per cent of grandparents (one in five) said they didn't use a child safety seat with their grandchildren, eight years and younger, when they were passengers in their car. Child safety seats, properly installed, can reduce the risk of death in motor-vehicle collisions by 69 per cent for infants and 47 per cent for toddlers.

Source: www.grandparenting.org

THE LAST WORD

These stories were written by grandparents and posted on the Internet. We have edited them for length.

Don't Go Near the Water

Recently our son and his wife invited us over to give our newborn grandson his first bath. We were thrilled but surprised when they informed us that we were expected to watch a video on "a new approach to bathing your baby" before we could proceed. We casually asked what could possibly be new under the sun about baths? They explained that the experts now recommend that babies be placed in water completely dressed and their clothing should be taken off one piece at a time.

As seasoned grandparents, we have patiently dealt with the "how-to" lists and tedious instructions of our three other kids when they became parents. Using a calm approach, we gently said that we would prefer to bathe the baby in the traditional manner, rather than watch the video. Their response still has me reeling. They said, "No video, no bath." This led to a first – grandparents being thrown out with the bathwater, rather than the baby!

Tricks and Treats

My son and his wife told me that their baby was to eat only healthy foods – no sugar, additives, or treat foods from day one. As my grandson's caregiver two days a week, I stuck by the drill. Adam and I spent the months together exploring the world, which of course included his introduction to my favourite health food – ice cream.

At Adam's first birthday party, his parents decided that he could have his first taste of ice cream. They made a big to-do about this being his first ice-cream treat. I thought to myself, "Well, what his parents don't know won't hurt them. Just then Adam looked right at me and said, "Grammy give me first ice cream." I was busted!

Teeth or Consequences

I was babysitting for my nine-month-old grandson, which became my best job after retiring as a fireman. Max Jr. somehow squirmed his way out of my arms and to my horror, he chipped his front tooth on a glass table. I rushed the baby to the hospital, terrified that he would never look right and that I had forever lost his parents' trust in me as their sitter. When the kids came and the doctor attended to Max, I was in such a high state of anxiety that they gently suggested I go home.

Later that evening, the pediatrician called me at home and said, "The baby is fine, but I'm worried about you!" Max is a teenager now and we still laugh about the day Grandpa was treated by his baby doctor.

Principle Ten

Take Care of You

The aging process has you firmly in its grasp if you never get the urge to throw a snowball.

— Doug Larson

Grandparenting takes energy. Like parenting, it requires us to seek out ways to balance how we look after others and ourselves. Effective grandparents are filled with vitality, an idea that speaks not only to our physical health, but to our emotional, intellectual, and spiritual well-being, as well.

Remaining vital and balanced doesn't necessarily mean giving equal time to all aspects of your life, but it does mean aligning your efforts with what matters most to you. That is why it is important to establish your vision and priorities as a grandparent up front (see Principle One).

Principle Ten is about taking care of your physical, emotional, and spiritual well-being. These three areas do not stand alone, but are interconnected in the way we live our day-to-day lives. The goal is not perfect health or living to age 110. By now, most of us are unwilling to forego the simple pleasures of life to gain two more years on the geriatric ward. It is about maintaining a quality of life that allows you to enjoy every day and to be the kind of grandparent you want to, and can realistically be.

The good news is that our grandchildren can actually help us achieve the balance and quality of life we seek. Being a grandparent promotes emotional well-being and is a source of spiritual fulfillment. Contrary to some new grandboomer's fears that the label signals "old and over-the-hill," grandparenting helps keep us young and vital. As centenarian George Burns once said, "You can't help getting older, but you don't have to get old."

THEN AND NOW

Happily, North Americans are living longer and healthier lives than ever before. This has two major implications for the boomer generation. First, we can expect to be healthy, active grandparents. Secondly, we need to be prepared at the same time to help our aging parents, who are also living longer.

While most boomers say they are in very good or excellent health, the Healthy Boomer Midlife Survey showed a clear disconnect between our psychosocial and physical health. Many midlife men and women suffer from insomnia, depression, low moods, migraines, and anxiety. Some, who have rejected the formal religion they learned as children, are on a quest to find the spiritual meaning of life and death. Those that are employed (especially women) are desperately seeking to find a balance in their lives that allows them more time for family, friends, and leisure pursuits.

While boomer women feel stressed about balancing work and home life, they are also the first generation of women to have been (largely) in control of their reproduction, education, and career choices. Most boomer grandmothers have more access to discretionary money and a personal car than their mothers did. They have more permission to talk about and deal with health issues such as menopause and depression.

Susan compares her experience of menopause with that of her mother's.

My mother never mentioned what she was going through. I always wondered why she was so unhappy when she was in her fifties, and why she did things like stand outside on the porch in her nightgown on cold mornings. Things are different now. I even joke with my teenage grandson about my hot flashes. I get a lot of support from my women friends and my physician. Menopause has become simply a stage in growing older, not a medical condition to be feared and hushed up.

Most boomer men are retiring in good health at younger ages than their fathers did. There have been dramatic declines in heart disease as a cause of early death in men and a downward turn in deaths from lung cancer – the leading cancer killer among aging men for many decades. Some midlife men are socially and emotionally prepared for retirement. Others are not – they feel isolated and depressed, having left the career that gave them identity, status, and day-to-day structure.

Despite overall improvements in our physical health, most boomers are aware that chronic diseases and annoying aches and pains start to show up after age fifty. The good news is that most of us have managed to quit smoking. The bad news is that we have gained weight. The result has been an increase in diabetes (especially among men) and arthritis (especially among women), as well as bothersome back, foot, and digestive problems that affect our mobility and energy levels.

Harry, a grandfather of six, shares his concern about how his health has been affected by weight gain and how it limits his capacity as a grandfather.

I was always prone to back problems, but since gaining fifty pounds it has become a chronic condition. I can't lift my grandchildren any more. It is difficult getting them in and out of a high chair, playing with them at the park, or even holding the baby for any length of time. I've resolved to lose the weight and have started a back-strengthening program at the YMCA. Before it didn't seem to matter so much because I sat in front of a computer all the time. But I don't want to miss out on being close to my grandchildren, and I don't want my own kids to see me as old and helpless.

BARRIERS TO TAKING CARE OF OURSELVES

For busy boomers the number-one barrier to putting this principle into practice is a lack of time. This is related to some of the other challenges discussed below.

I am too tired to look after me.

When we come home from work exhausted and have to face another shift of housework and family responsibilities, it is no wonder we feel too tired to add more activities to our daily schedules. Ironically, it is physical activity, meditation, and spending time with our grandchildren that rejuvenate us.

David and Mary, who have three grandchildren, made some simple but important changes in their life patterns that helped them renew their energy.

> We were caught in a vicious circle that just made us more and more tired. After working late we'd have wine with dinner, then I'd collapse in front of the TV with a nightcap. Mary would inevitably find herself falling asleep answering personal e-mails or doing catch-up office work. On weekends we would run around frenetically trying to do all of our errands, entertain, and see our children and grandchildren. Finally, we decided not to drink between Monday and Friday and to take a walk after dinner every evening. I started to sleep better and felt less fatigued almost immediately. Then my son asked if I could take my grandson Jason to soccer on Saturday afternoons. I felt energized being with Jason and his friends. They made me laugh and feel alive. Mary and I decided to ditch half of our weekend errands and get in the habit of making Saturday afternoon our time with one or more of our grandkids. There is no question

in my mind. These changes have made a big difference in my energy levels.

I've always put myself last.
Many grandparents devote themselves to making life easier and more rewarding for their children. Sometimes this extends to others in their family, workplace, and community. They are used to putting others' needs ahead of their own. This is not a bad thing, in itself. Indeed, there is strong evidence that altruistic people are generally happy people . . . and that they make the best grandparents. The problem arises when this ingrained attitude stops people from taking charge of their own well-being. They forget that the aging body and mind is not as forgiving as when they were thirty. They neglect themselves physically, emotionally, and spiritually at a time in life when they are vulnerable to health problems.

Elizabeth, who became a grandmother at age fifty-three, talks about her decision to slow down and pay more attention to her own emotional and physical needs.

> I did the math and figured that my life was about two-thirds done. Most of it was spent putting other people's needs before my own physical and mental health. I still want to give to other people, especially my new grandbaby. But I also realize that I have to take time to take care of me; to speak up for what I need in my personal relationships and lifestyle.

The damage is done. I have always hated exercise. I love to indulge in good food and wine. I'm too old to change my lifestyle now.
This is the oldest and lamest excuse in the book. Millions of North Americans have proven that it is *never* too late to make changes in our lifestyles. Consider this: more than 50 per cent of middle-aged Canadian men who were regular smokers have quit, despite the fact that nicotine

is a highly addictive product. Millions of older men and women have improved their eating patterns, lost weight, and taken up physical activity, often after age sixty. While it is true that lifestyle patterns established in childhood affect health in later life, it is also true that quitting smoking can start to reverse the damage almost immediately, whether you are twenty-five, fifty-five, or seventy-five. Losing excess weight combined with increases in moderate physical activity can lower high blood pressure and reduce one's risk for diabetes and some cancers at any age.

Dr. Miroslava Lhotsky, a physician who specializes in midlife health, explains that the secret is to start now by making small changes, not trying to change everything all at once.

> Most people cycle through several stages when they make lifestyle changes, moving from thinking about it and making up roadblocks through to action and maintenance of the new behaviour. Most of us slip back from time to time. This is okay. We need to give ourselves permission to make mistakes and to learn from them. You will eventually succeed as long as you persist and take it one small step at a time.

I feel guilty when I say no.

Some of the grandparents we spoke with said that they feel guilty, even apprehensive, if they say no to a request to babysit or help out with their grandchildren. This is especially the case when there are tensions with in-laws or after a separation or divorce. They know that their grandchildren need them and they worry that one of the parents may limit access if they feel hurt or abandoned. These are honest and real concerns, but feeling guilty does not help the situation. It may only add to the trouble, as explained by Cathy, a grandmother of eight who lives alone.

> After her divorce, my daughter was made the custodial parent. She relied heavily on me to mind the children, especially when she had

to travel out of town. It was too much for me, but I never said no. I felt guilty. Had my daughter repeated the same mistakes in her relationship that I had? What kind of mother would deny her daughter and darling grandchildren when they needed her so much?

Our relationship began to deteriorate. Imagine how shocked I was when my daughter told me to "stop acting like a martyr." Guilt and silence had made things worse. I *was* acting like a martyr. I should have been more honest about my own needs from the start.

My grandmother wasn't expected to be the kind of Super Gram you write about in this book. I'm angry about all of the demands on me. I'm tired of trying to do it all.

As women who have lived through an era that expected us to be "Super Moms," as well as super partners and super employees, the last thing we want to do is suggest that we all must now be "Super Grams." And we are the first to admit that we are not. As pioneers in women's rights, female boomers and the society we helped create have always had high expectations for what we can accomplish. Some midlife women feel that they and their families have suffered as a result of trying to be superwomen. Karen explains how becoming a grandmother has given her an opportunity to rethink her expectations for herself.

I have finally stopped listening to the past pressures that society put on my generation, and I put on myself, to be super at everything. I have decided to approach grandmothering in a kinder, gentler way. I may not be the perfect grandmother. I may make mistakes. But that is okay because the important thing is unconditional love, not rushing around trying to be everything to everybody. This approach gives me peace and contentment. My grandchildren sense this. They know that they can relax with me and just be themselves.

TAKING CARE OF YOUR PHYSICAL, EMOTIONAL, AND SPIRITUAL WELL-BEING

Physical Well-Being

Grandparenting is not for sissies. Keeping up with active grandchildren requires stamina and energy. It takes physical strength and patience, as any grandparent who has held a toddler up to a light switch for ten minutes so they can delight in turning it off and on can attest.

There is an expectation among boomers, the journalists who write about them, and the marketers who sell to them, that our generation will be more physically involved with our grandchildren than our grandparents were. The Big Generation is expert at playing (and some would say indulging). We are healthier than our predecessors and bent on rediscovering the joys of active play, nature, and travel with our grandchildren.

Nancy says that having grandchildren has helped her and her husband make better decisions about how they themselves eat, sleep, and stay active.

> We want to be good role models, and of course we want our grand-children to be as healthy as possible. So when we are together, we make a point of sitting down to healthy meals and having healthy snacks. We go to bed shortly after them instead of staying up with the TV, and we do active things like swimming with them. It carries over when they are not here. I find myself reaching for an apple instead of a piece of pie and going to bed thirty minutes earlier.

Some grandboomers live with activity limitations as a result of chronic diseases or injuries. They can still be vital and healthy people who bring wonder and comfort into their grandchildren's lives.

Ron, who has lived with cerebral palsy since he was a child, is a role model for both his children and his grandchildren. They have watched his physical health deteriorate gradually over the years, but his wit and emotional involvement have remained the same. His son talks about how Ron grandparents so effectively from a wheelchair.

Dad phones my twelve-year-old daughter, Susan, at least once a week and they have long conversations about her school work, her friends, and their philosophies on life. They also e-mail a lot and he helps her with school projects on the computer. He makes her type in the work so she will learn spelling and punctuation, even though he has software that permits him to speak into his computer. Susan says he is the best listener in the whole world. He shows up at all her special events. Being in a wheelchair is never an obstacle to his being a great granddad.

Emotional Well-Being

There is no doubt that grandparenting is an enormous source of joy and emotional well-being. All of the grandparents we spoke with talked about how wonderful it is to share a grandchild's sense of imagination and fun, in a unique emotional relationship that is quite different from parenting. Margaret, a grandmother of eight, describes it this way.

Each time I hold a new grandbaby and bathe and change him, I fall in love all over again. The relationship is intense and intimate but different than it was with my own children. It feels lighter and easier. My only real responsibilities are to love and support my grandchildren. The parents have the harder job of raising them twenty-four hours a day. I am there to be a friend, a mentor, a fan, and a playmate. My older grandchildren make me laugh out loud. I feel rejuvenated and happy when we are together.

Margaret's husband, Jack, gets enormous satisfaction from knowing that he is sharing a sense of family history and belonging with his grandchildren.

I think that grandparents can help their grandchildren feel rooted and connected to a family that has pride, traditions, and a loving attitude. My grandmother did that for me. She made my ancestors and our family traditions come alive for me. I knew I came from a family that loved and respected children, and took pride in the accomplishments of hard work. It feels really good to be able to pass these values on to my grandchildren.

Grandparenting contributes to our emotional well-being in many ways. Helping us "be in the moment" is particularly important. Being in the here and now, right now, allows us to be truly aware of what and who is around us. Dr. Jon Kabat-Zinn, who calls this "mindfulness," has taught thousands of patients in his Stress Reduction Program at the University of Massachusetts Medical Center to relax through meditation that allows you to be in the moment. By capturing the present and living fully within each moment as it happens, one can reduce anxiety, achieve inner peace, and enrich the quality of life.

Jane, whose granddaughter Ella was visiting for a week, talks eloquently about how grandparenting offers a second chance at being present in the moment.

Did I appreciate and concentrate on my own two children as much as I do on this wonderful baby, Ella? Every moment with her is so precious, so delightful. I look at her and think that perhaps I was so busy taking care of all the practical things for my babies that I didn't slow down enough to just love them the way I do my granddaughter. My daughter-in-law, Leslie, said something very touching to me. She said, "You are obviously just as much in love with my daughter as I am."

Leslie is right; it feels the same . . . the anticipation to see her; the terrible sorrow and sadness when I leave her; the hurt I feel when she cries; the love I feel just watching her. Will I feel the same about the grandchildren to follow? I believe I will, and that is a glorious feeling. This is truly a wonderful time of life.

All of us want grandparenting to be a joyful experience. That is why it is so important to be honest with ourselves, and to acknowledge that overload, fatigue, anxiety, depression, and relationship issues are common in midlife. It is okay to say that visits are too long, or you are not prepared to babysit three grandchildren at once, or that you simply need some time off. Feeling exploited is bad for you and everyone else. When grandboomers are honest and able to say no, many emotional issues can be avoided.

Grandchildren can add to stress or relieve it, especially if you make an effort to put aside your preoccupations with other concerns when you are with them. Mary Jane recounts how grandchildren are more observant about this than we think.

I was sitting on the sidelines at my grandson's soccer game, chatting with his mother and watching the game. Torin seemed to be oblivious to us, as he seldom looked over. At the end, when I complimented him on his playing, he said, "But you weren't even watching, you were talking to Mommy." I was a bit taken aback, but was able to recount specific plays he had made. He seemed relieved and pleased that I had paid attention – at least some of the time. This was a good lesson for Grandma!

Spiritual Well-Being

Grandparenthood comes at a time when we are also looking for more meaning in our lives, when we are looking beyond our own material needs and wanting to connect and contribute to a larger community. Carl Jung said, "We seek to define ourselves and succeed as individuals in the first half of our life . . . in the second half of life we reach for psychospiritual wholeness."

The research conducted by Peggy and her colleagues for their second book, *The Juggling Act*, suggests that many boomers are confused and undecided about spirituality. Some are in the process of rediscovering their religious roots; others are exploring new options. For most of the respondents in the Healthy Boomer Midlife Survey, spirituality was not about formal religion, but a sense of connection to some higher power, and a belief in something greater than themselves. Many spoke about experiencing spirituality in nature, and in connecting with others in the forms of altruism, friendship, and social action.

Spiritual well-being becomes increasingly important in midlife when we must face our own mortality as older family members and friends our own age die. Painful as this may be, it forces us to deal with spiritual issues, and to forgive old wounds that get in the way of achieving a sense of wholeness.

Grandparents and grandchildren share a unique interest and opportunity to explore the spiritual side of life. Virtually all cultures and religions place an emphasis on this role. For example, most Native American and Canadian aboriginal communities see sharing spiritual wisdom and experience as the primary role of grandparents. Arthur Kornhaber suggests that one of the key roles of grandparents is to model how to live a good life and values such as love, compassion, joy, peace, gentleness, kindness, and honesty. He has shown in his research on grandparenting that spiritual teachings, usually expressed in religion, are most easily passed on from grandparents to grandchild. Grandchildren see their grandparents going to church, synagogue, or mosque, and observe them practising their religion in everyday ways. This is still the case for many families in North America.

However, the 2002 Grandparenting Survey carried out by the American Association of Retired Persons (AARP) showed that grandboomers are less likely than their predecessors to spend time with their grandchildren dealing with spiritual and religious matters. Similarly, the grandparents we talked with ranked "teaching moral and spiritual values" near the bottom of a list of twelve potential grandparenting roles. It appears that many boomers are unprepared to define or even describe their role as grandparents when it comes to this sensitive issue.

Whether or not you believe in religion or spirituality, be prepared for questions about these things. Children are naturally curious about spiritual issues, and because many modern families shy away from these matters, they are highly likely to ask you about death, God, heaven, and hell. Some grandchildren will even have their own theories, which they will be anxious to share with you.

Peggy describes how wonderful it was when two of her grandsons comforted her after her dad died.

> One of them told me not to worry, that heaven was made up of thousands of "black holes" in outer space – one for each species. Grampa had gone to the one for humans. God would never make a mistake and send him to the wrong place, like the black hole for skunks or giraffes. A second grandson piped up, "Yeah, and the human heaven is filled with great golf courses that are all free. In fact, Grampa is probably playing a game there right now."

When grandchildren ask questions about spirituality, you don't need to have all of the answers or embark on a lecture. The important thing is to let them know that their questions are important, and that it is good to be curious about life and our place within it.

If you are involved in an organized religion, show your grandchild how you practise your faith in everyday life, not just on holy days. Associate religion with joy and kindness, not guilt and boredom. Grandparents who have abandoned organized religion can still appreciate the spiritual aspects of nature, peace, and the circle of life: the magic and wonder of a pollywog turning into a frog, of the unique architecture of every snowflake, of a baby brother or sister being born. You can attend to these things with your grandchildren and encourage them to look for answers you may not have. Who knows – you might even look for those answers together.

ARE YOU READY FOR SPIRITUAL SERENITY?

Kathryn D. Cramer, author of *Roads Home: Seven Pathways to Midlife Wisdom*, discusses six signs that you are ready for spiritual serenity. You begin to:

- take more time to reflect on the meaning of life;
- feel upset over injustices in the world;
- long to better accept your personal beliefs about death;
- struggle to understand why good people suffer;
- seek a more satisfying life philosophy;
- yearn for more solitude and silence.

QUESTIONS AND ANSWERS

Q: My husband died last year and my grandchildren aged six and four were upset and confused. We talked a lot but it was hard to explain death to them. Now I am worried that they will lose their memories of their grandpa. Is there anything I can do to keep his memory alive for them?

A: Even very young children mourn the loss of a beloved grandparent, a fact that often goes unnoticed by the grieving spouse and children of the deceased. Experts suggest that we include children at funerals and talk openly with them about death, sharing their sadness and responding to their questions as best you can. You can keep their grandfather's memory alive by looking at photographs and telling stories about his life and your family. Don't be afraid to take your grandchildren to visit his grave. Graveyards are wonderful, peaceful places for walking, talking, exploring, and sharing your love.

Q: I am struggling to find some balance in my life: to find time to look after me, to carry on a full-time job, and to be there for my husband, mother, children, and grandchildren. I feel constantly frazzled. Any suggestions?

A: Ironically, slowing down and pacing yourself may be one of the best remedies for life in the fast lane. You cannot do it all, so make a list of your priorities and what you can realistically do in a day or a week or a month. Schedule in time for you – to rest, recreate, and take some time outs. Let go of some of the "busywork" outside of your main priorities. Slowing down has some natural consequences – the heart rate slows, the mind calms, and we become more present in the moment.

WHAT THE RESEARCH TELLS US

Some Highlights from the Healthy Boomer Midlife Survey

- While 83 per cent of boomer respondents ranked their health as "excellent," "very good," or "good," 68 per cent had or were experiencing depression (acute or occasional), 33 per cent were experiencing insomnia, and 20 per cent were experiencing anxiety.
- When asked if they had health problems that interfered with their day-to-day functioning, 64 per cent said "no" and 26 per cent said "yes."
- When asked about their plans to retire, 48 per cent said they would retire gradually, 19 per cent all at once, 21 per cent not at all, and 12 per cent were undecided.
- Sixty-five per cent of respondents said they are *not* comfortable with their current weight.

Source: Edwards, P., M. Lhotsky, and J. Turner. *The Juggling Act: The Healthy Boomer's Guide to Achieving Balance in Midlife.* Toronto: McClelland & Stewart Ltd, 2002.

Grandchildren Benefit Too

Children with loving and involved grandparents feel emotionally secure. They have a positive image of aging and look forward to becoming grandparents themselves one day. Children with close relationships speak enthusiastically about the sense of joyfulness and fun they share with their grandparents.

Source: Kornhaber, A., and K. Woodward. *Grandparents/Grandchildren: The Vital Connection.* Garden City, NY: Doubleday, 1981.

THE LAST WORD

Over the course of writing this book, we were sent many special quotes about grandparenting. Here are some of our favourites:

"Grandmotherhood does not give us the right to speak without thinking, but only the right to think without speaking." – *Lois Wyse*

"The closest friends I have made all through life have been people who also grew up close to a loved and loving grandmother or grandfather." – *Margaret Mead*

"Grandparents are always being told that they are living history to their grandchildren, that they give the children the reassurance of their roots. For me and many grandmothers I have talked to, it works the other way as well. They give us continuity." – *Ruth Goode*

"My grandmother started walking five miles a day when she was sixty. She's ninety-seven now, and we don't know where the hell she is." – *Ellen DeGeneres*

"I was an angel in her eyes, no matter what the facts were, no matter what anyone else happened to think." – *Judy Langford Carter*

"There is a delight, a comfort, an easing of the burden, a renewal of joy in my own life, to feel the stream of life of which I am a part going on like this." – *Betty Friedan*

"Being a grandfather is stepping out into the dawn." – *Victor Hugo*

"When I die, I want to die like my grandmother who died peacefully in her sleep. Not screaming like all the passengers in her car." – *Author Unknown*

Conclusion

It is evident that we must extend ourselves to embrace and advocate for all children. There is no such thing as somebody else's grandchildren.

— Dr. Lillian Carson

None of us are perfect – our grandchildren don't expect it, nor do their parents. We can be the grandparents we want to be, maybe not all the time, but hopefully most of the time. Regardless of whether you are a hands-on grandparent living close by or a more distant one in another city, applying the ten principles for intentional grand-parenting will make your experience and that of your grandchildren and their parents more satisfying and enjoyable.

This chapter reminds us that we are not alone, that we need to reach out to other grandparents – both those that are part of our extended families and those we do not yet know. The baby boomers are the largest generation ever to be born in North America. We wield both market and political clout. This provides us with an enormous oppor-tunity to make things better for children and young families.

YOU ARE NOT ALONE
Other books about grandparenting talk about the pitfalls in a large network of numerous grandparents. There is potential for competition, feeling neglected, or simply never getting to know your grandchildren's other grandparents. We authors have not found this to be true, even

though in Peggy's extended family there are already fourteen grandparents and ten great-grandparents. On the contrary, grandchildren have helped to bring the network of grandparents together. We meet at baptisms and school events and have visited each other's houses in different cities when our grandchildren and their parents are there. The tension associated with divorce and remarriage become irrelevant when the grandchildren are the focus of our attention.

Obviously, you are likely to become more friendly with some in-laws than others. Mary Jane and Michael, who have much in common with their daughter-in-law's parents, Dick and Bonnie, have struck up a special friendship.

> We share some special occasions including Thanksgiving at Dick and Bonnie's cottage, and this summer the four of us joined our adult children and grandchildren at a summer camp for a week. This makes it easy for everyone. The parents get a real holiday, our grandchildren get time with four doting grandparents, and we as couples also get time to ourselves. Not to mention the laughs and good times. Who else but another set of grandparents is going to want to sit and talk about how wonderful their grandchildren are?

One of the hottest issues for new grandparents is what they are to be called, especially when there are multiple grandparents. How are the children to distinguish between all their grandmas and grandpas? There are Web sites listing common (and not-so-common) names for grandparents, and it is a frequent topic of discussion in grandparent chat groups.

Some grandparents insist on certain names. We believe that grandparents should tell family members their preference for a name, but also be open to what their adult children and grandchildren want to call them. Often, the grandchildren decide by default when they invent a name because they cannot pronounce the name you or others have chosen. For example, Lynn's granddaughter Samar calls her and her husband Gawa and Bampa. "It's close enough for me!" says Lynn.

Jackie, whose grandparenting name is "Nana," was surprised when one day her granddaughter called her "Oma," which is the name she uses for her other grandmother.

> At first I was a bit taken aback – even jealous – when she mistakenly called me Oma. Then I thought about how kind and energetic Oma is. I realized it's not so bad for my young granddaughter to make such a mistake. In a way, it's a kind of compliment.

The old axiom "Friends are good medicine" becomes especially important as we grow older. Our lifelong friends will still be there when our grandchildren grow up and no longer have as much time for us. Some of our friends have watched our children grow and it is such fun to share the joy of grandparenting with them. It does not matter if they are not grandparents themselves. Indeed, many people in midlife who do not have children or grandchildren of their own are looking for opportunities to interact with children. There may also be opportunities to get together with friends who had children later in life, as is the case with Peggy and her friend Wendy.

> I was twenty-two when I had my daughter Patty and she was nineteen when she had her first child. My friend Wendy was in her forties when she had Dylan. So we are able to get together with kids the same age, even though one is a son and the others are grandchildren.

While good friends are patient and will (mostly) indulge our passion for our grandchildren, they have limits as well. Beware of being the grandparent-bore and be sure to nurture and protect your friendships in their own right as well.

THE GIVE-AND-TAKE BETWEEN PARENTS
AND THEIR ADULT CHILDREN

Grandparents had an honoured place in pre-industrial and indige-nous cultures. Grandmothers were celebrated for their wisdom, permanence, and even mystical powers. They played key roles as teachers and caregivers while the parents had children and worked hard to feed the family. Grandfathers were the patriarchs and most families lived in multi-generational households, where wives and children were dependent on the grandfather for assets and land inheritance.

All of this has changed. Generations within families are no longer dependent on each other for financial or physical survival. So what is the role grandboomers can play now and what is the legacy we can leave behind for future generations?

Freed from the constraints of the past, we grandboomers can build relationships with our grandchildren and adult children that revolve around loving, caring, and interdependence. Changes in marriage, the economy, work, and family structures have made grandparents more important than ever. We welcome the roles of nurturer, fan, mentor, historian, and supporter.

Principle Two describes how grandparents can best support their adult children in the parenting role. How can young parents recipro-cate? Here are some ideas from the grandparents we talked to:

1. Listen to my ideas about the kind of grandparent I would like to be. Tell me your hopes and expectations.
2. Be gentle if I give advice. I am only trying to be helpful.
3. Give me feedback. Let me know when things are going well and when you would like me to do something differently.
4. Tell me how you want me to handle delicate situations such as temper tantrums or acting out when your daughter or son is in my care.

5. Ask ahead of time when you would like me to babysit. Respect the fact that I have other commitments and that I need some private space too.

6. Share the small everyday details about my grandchild – that he is beginning to crawl, that he read a "chapter" book, that she is collecting things related to frogs, that you are working on toilet training. This helps me stay up to date and gives me relevant ways to connect with my grandchild.

7. Include me in family outings, rituals, and get-togethers. Invite me to school concerts, recitals, and sports events where my grandchild is involved. Next to you, I am her biggest fan!

8. Keep my photo on display in your home and tell my grandchild about me and our family.

9. Respect the special relationship I have with my grandchild. It is different than the relationship you have with him. Help us find opportunities to be together.

10. Ask for help when you need it. I know that bringing up a family is one of the most challenging jobs in life. Unless you tell me, I may not see the need to give you additional practical or emotional support.

11. Be honest with my grandchild if I am sick or in need of comfort. Help us share some quiet but meaningful time together. Being with a young person I love is the best tonic there is!

12. Remember that my excitement over your child is an extension of my love for you. Now that you are a father or mother, you will learn that a parent's love lasts forever.

GRANDPARENTS UNITE!

Grandboomers have the potential to advocate and influence on behalf of children and young families. Many boomers are in positions of influence in our communities and nations. Grandparent power is just beginning!

There is clear evidence that policies and programs that support parents and children are effective. One example is the Perry Preschool Project – an American program of early childcare and education for children at high-risk for school failure and delinquency. Researchers followed the Perry Preschool graduates till age twenty-seven, comparing them to a similar group of children who lacked early enrichment. By the time the two groups were twenty-seven years old, 33 per cent more of the Perry graduates had finished high school, 80 per cent fewer had been arrested, only half as many had been on welfare at any time during the preceding decade, and 42 per cent fewer of the Perry girls got pregnant as teenagers. The research estimated that every dollar invested in the project saved the government $7.16 because of lower medical, remedial education, crime control, and welfare costs.

You may be a privileged grandparent whose successful adult children are raising happy, healthy children with brilliant futures. But as a group, we cannot afford to ignore children and families that need more help than even grandparents can provide. We need to actively encourage government policies and community programs that support parents and grandparents, parenting skills, and healthy child development. If we truly believe children are the future, we must work together to ensure that all of them get off to the best possible start.

FOR THE JOY OF IT!

Arthur Kornhaber suggests that grandparenting is part of a significant new phase of life he calls "continuity." It is characterized by increased emotional, intellectual, and spiritual maturity, self-confidence, and an increasingly selfless orientation in life. But most importantly, grandparenting offers us the chance to experience joy in our day-to-day lives. It's such a grand thing to be a parent of a parent – that's why the world calls us GRANDparents. Enjoy!

Appendix

To Learn More

ABOUT GRANDPARENTING

Books

Bosak, Susan. *How to Build the Grandma Connection.* Whitechurch-
   Stouffville, ON: The Communication Project, 2000.
Canfield, Jack et al. *Chicken Soup for the Grandparent's Soul.* Deerfield
   Beach, FL: Health Communications, Inc., 2002.
Carlson, Ron. *The Don't Sweat Guide for Grandparents.* New York:
   Hyperion, 2001.
Carson, Lillian. *The Essential Grandparent: A Guide to Making a
   Difference.* Deerfield Beach, FL: Health Communications, Inc., 1996.
——. *The Essential Grandparent's Guide to Divorce: Making a Difference
   in the Family.* Deerfield Beach, FL: Health Communications, Inc.,
   1999.
Kornhaber, Arthur. *The Grandparent Guide: The Definitive Guide to
   Coping with the Challenges of Modern Grandparenting.* New York:
   McGraw-Hill, 2002.
Kornhaber, Arthur, and K.L. Woodward. *Grandparents-Grandchildren:
   The Vital Connection.* New York: Doubleday, 1981.
Wasserman, Selma. *The Long-Distance Grandmother: How to Stay
   Close to Distant Children.* Vancouver, BC: Hartley & Marks, 1996.

Westheimer, Dr. Ruth, and Dr. Steven Kaplan. *Grandparenthood*. New
    York: Routledge, 2000.
Wyse, Lois, and L. Rogers. *Funny, You Don't Look Like a Grandmother*.
    New York: Crown Publishers, Inc., 1989.
Zullo, Kathryn, and Allan Zullo. *The Nanas and the Papas: A Boomer's
    Guide to Grandparenting*. Kansas City, MI: Andrews McMeel
    Publishing, 1998.

Web sites and Organizations

Foundation for Grandparenting: **www.grandparenting.org**
Founded by grandparenting pioneer Arthur Kornhaber, this organization provides education, information, a newsletter, and networking.

The National Grandparent Information Center: **www.aarp.org**
The best grandparenting site going is part of the larger Web site of the
American Association of Retired Persons (AARP). The site contains
articles, links to support groups, research, and a message board to
share your stories.

Grandboomers: **www.grandboomers.com**
Jane Murphy and Marc Jasmin created this site especially for
grandboomers. It contains letters, articles, and book reviews for and
by boomers.

Grandparents Magazine: **www.grandparentsmagazine.net**
Katrina Hayday Wester created this on-line resource "to keep grandparents cool and hip." The site features product reviews, activity ideas,
articles, and message forums.

Grandparent World: **www.grandparentworld.com**
This site was created by grandparents for grandparents and is edited
by a group headed by a grandmother with sixteen grandchildren. It

provides advice on shopping and travelling with grandchildren, health, and what's new in grandparenting.

The Essential Grandparent: **www.essentialgrandparent.com**
On this site psychotherapist and author Dr. Lillian Carson answers questions about grandparenting and provides an opportunity to join The Essential Grandparent Reading Circle, a group designed to share ideas and experiences about reading to children.

ABOUT CHILD ÐEVELOPMENT, PARENTING, AND FAMILIES

Books

Brooks, Robert, and Sam Goldstein. *Raising Resilient Children.* New York: McGraw-Hill, 2001.

Canadian Medical Association. *Complete Book of Mother and Child Care.* Dorling Kindersley, 2002.

Coloroso, Barbara. *Kids Are Worth It!* Toronto: Penguin Canada, 1994, 2001.

Covey, Steven. *The 7 Habits of Highly Effective Families.* New York: Golden Books, 1997.

Douglas, Ann. *The Mother of All Parenting Books.* Etobicoke, ON: John Wiley & Sons Canada Ltd., 2003.

Elias, Maurice, Steven Tobias, and Brian Friedlander. *Emotionally Intelligent Parenting.* New York: Three Rivers Press, 1999.

Hallowell, Edward. *The Childhood Roots of Adult Happiness.* Toronto: Random House, 2002.

Hogg, Tracy, and Melinda Blau. *Secrets of the Baby Whisperer.* New York: Ballantyne Books, 2002.

Langlois, Christine. *Raising Healthy Children. Raising Great Kids: Ages 6 to 12. Canadian Living* magazine.

Maisel, Roberta. *All Grown Up: Living Happily Ever After With Your Adult Children*. Gabriola Island, BC: New Society Publishers, 2001.

Seligman, Martin. *Learned Optimism*. New York: Pocket Books, Simon & Schuster Inc., 1990, 1998.

——. *The Optimistic Child*. New York: HarperCollins Publishers Inc., 1995.

Shapiro, Lawrence. *How to Raise a Child with a High EQ*. New York: HarperCollins Publishers Inc., 2003.

Web sites and Organizations

Children Youth & Families Education & Research Network: **www.cyfernet.org**
This site draws on the resources from universities across the country to provide practical, research-based information on children, youth, and families. Topics include child and youth development, parenting, grandparenting, and family information, research reports, evaluation tools, bibliographies, and more.

Motherisk: **www.motherisk.org**
This is a very comprehensive Web site associated with the Hospital for Sick Children in Toronto. It has lots of information about the safety or risk of drugs, chemicals, and disease during pregnancy and lactation.

Today's Parent: **www.todaysparent.com**
This Web site for *Today's Parent* magazine offers information surrounding child development, parenting, and family life. Additional features include scheduled on-line chats with experts, parenting forums, and a craft corner.

Growing Healthy Canadians: **www.growinghealthykids.com**
This Web site is based on a framework that focuses on the life transitions children go through, and the positive outcomes we would like to

see all children achieve. It shows how families, schools, communities, workplaces, and governments can help achieve these positive outcomes.

Child Development Institute: **www.childdevelopmentinfo.com**
An award-winning site for information on child development and parenting. Recommended by *Psychology Today* and the American Psychological Association.

Invest in Kids: **www.investinkids.ca**
Extremely comprehensive. Invest in Kids is a national charitable organization dedicated to ensuring the healthy social, emotional, and intellectual development of children from birth to age five. The Web site includes articles, research results, and recommendations for good toys and products for kids. Their motto is "The years before five last the rest of their lives."

Zero to Three: **www.zerotothree.org**
This Web site is a leading resource on early child development maintained by a national, non-profit organization. You can enter the site as a parent or professional to access comprehensive information on the early years.

Public Health Agency of Canada, Division of Childhood and Adolescence: **www.phac-aspc.gc.ca/dca-dea**
The Division of Childhood and Adolescence is the federal government's focal point on the health of children and youth, families, and parenting. Click on the Centres of Excellence for Children's Well-being and explore the sections on family, parenting, and specific age groups.

Canadian Institute of Child Health: **www.cich.ca**
This reliable non-profit organization has an excellent resources section and extensive links to other good organizations committed to healthy child development.

Family TLC: **www.familytlc.net**
This site, which was created by early childhood educators, provides
busy, caring adults with a means to encourage learning and enrich
relationships with their children and grandchildren. The site contains
parenting tips, articles, and ideas for family activities.

ABOUT SAFETY AND ACTIVE PLAY

For information about safe toys and child products, visit:

- U.S Consumer Products Safety Commission: **www.cpsc.gov**
- National Association of State Public Interest Research Groups
  in partnership with the U.S. Consumer Product Safety
  Commission: **www.pirg.org/toysafety**
- Health Canada: **www.hc-sc.gc.ca/english/iyh/products/toys.html**
- Child and Family Canada: **www.cfc-efc.ca/menu/safety_en.htm**

For more information on active play in the community and in
schools, visit:

- Canada's Physical Activity Guides for Children and Youth:
  www.hc-sc.gc.ca/hppb/paguide/child_youth/index.html
- Alberta Centre for Active Living: **www.centre4activeliving.ca**
- Canadian Association Health Physical Education, Recreation
  and Dance (quality daily physical education in schools):
  www.cahperd.ca/e/qdpe/index.htm
- American Alliance for Health, Physical Education, Recreation
  and Dance: **www.aahperd.org**
- Go for Green: **www.goforgreen.ca**

ABOUT MIDLIFE HEALTH (Take care of you!)

Edwards, Peggy, M. Lhotsky, and J. Turner. *The Healthy Boomer: A No-Nonsense Midlife Health Guide for Women and Men.* Toronto: McClelland & Stewart Ltd., 1999.

——. *The Juggling Act: The Healthy Boomer's Guide to Achieving Balance in Midlife.* Toronto: McClelland & Stewart Ltd., 2002.

ABOUT CYBER-GRANDPARENTING

The following advice is not meant to be comprehensive, just a few ticklers and Web sites to get you going.

If you want to create a **family Web page**, contact your Internet service provider to see if they include a Web page hosting service. Most include it in the package you have already purchased. Once you have the space, you need to create a Web page on your computer, and then load it onto the hosting service. You can create a simple Web page in Microsoft Word or you can purchase software such as Dreamweaver, GoLive, Home Page, Page Mill, Cool Page, etc. There's a lot available, as a quick search of the Internet will demonstrate.

If you own an Apple computer, their .Mac service will provide you with an extremely simple means of creating a Web page and publishing it for anyone (including Windows users) to see.

Another alternative is to use a free Web hosting service. There are many choices and they are absolutely free with no obligation to purchase anything. Have a look at Freeservers or Freeweb or do a search on Google. Some hosting services may include advertising on your Web page; try to choose one that doesn't. Yahoo has a service in which you can post your photographs on-line so your family can see them. If they want a print of one of the pictures they can simply click on it and order it on-line from Yahoo.

There are many makes and varieties of **digital cameras**. Most are small and you just have to point and shoot. We can't advise which one you should purchase, but when looking consider whether the camera includes software that will easily permit you to manipulate your photographs on your computer. If you are a Mac user you are in luck. iPhoto is free Apple software that helps you organize your photographs on your computer. It will also create slideshows or even photo albums that can be printed for you by Apple.

If you want to buy a **scanner** there are many on the market, some less than $100. They are easy to set up and simple to use. Only buy an expensive scanner if you plan to print out the photos you scan in.

Internet video conferencing is in its infancy and might require some fiddling to get it to work smoothly. You will need a Webcam camera or, if you are a Mac user the iSight camera will work perfectly. Microsoft MSN messenger, Yahoo messenger, AOL instant messenger, or iChat for Mac will all work. Best to find someone who is computer literate to help you with this.

If you simply want to "chat" on-line, without using a camera to transmit images of yourself while you talk, you use the software mentioned in the previous paragraph. If you are only "chatting," they are very simple to use. Once you and your grandchild are both "on-line," you can type on your computer and he or she will immediately see it on his or her computer screen. It's quite fun to do and certainly has an immediacy that e-mail lacks.

There are many software packages you can purchase for creating a **family tree**. Do a search on the Web and you will find titles such as Legacy Family Tree, Ancestry Family Tree, Family Tree Journal, etc. If you find one you like, you should be able to download a free trial version of the software. Many of the packages provide you with advice on how to research your family tree and find your ancestors. Building a family tree will give your grandchildren a sense of where they came from and an understanding of family traditions.

If the description of **blogs** in Principle Eight whetted your appetite to become a grandblogger, you can simply begin keeping a chronological journal on the Web site you create. If you haven't created a Web site and have a strong urge to blog, you can blog for free at blogger.com or tblog.com. There is even free software to help you create a stunning design for your blog – try Moveable Type or Greymatter (yes, this really is the name of the software).

And finally, if you want to try playing **games** with your grandchild on the Web just ask what his or her favourite game is. Usually you can download a trial version before you buy it. It might make an interesting gift. Have fun.

NOTE TO OUR READERS

Web sites often change and new books are always being published. Please e-mail us at grandma@aldergroup.com if any of these Web sites disappear or if you discover new Web sites or books that you find useful.